I0140409

Reflections of a

GODDESS

The Awakening

S.R HARDING

Copyright © 2016 BHEE LLC

All rights reserved.

Printed and Bound in the United States By BHEE LLC

First Edition First Printing

All rights reserved. No part of this book may be reproduced or used in any

manner without the express written permission of the publisher.

SRHarding.com

Cover Illustration Copyright © 2016 by BHEE LLC

Cover design by RS Design Place www.rsdesignplace.com

Editing by Meredith Spangler

Video by Jason Harvey VIP Studios www.VIP-CO.com

ISBN: 978-0-9976976-0-5

This is a work of fiction. Names, characters, businesses, places, events and

incidents are either the products of the author's imagination or used in a

fictitious manner. Any resemblance to actual persons, living or dead, or

actual events is purely coincidental.

DEDICATION

In memory of my son Jaron Travis Gonzalez,
you will always be my sunshine.

CONTENTS

ACKNOWLEDGMENTS

This book would not have been possible without the support and encouragement of my husband, Tom. To my family that supported me and encouraged me to persevere, thank you. To my Mom and Aunt Bennie thank you for showing me how to be a strong woman. To my sister Bennie for listening to my rants, keeping me focused and always encouraging me to finish. Words cannot express my gratitude to my editor for the professional advice and assistance in polishing this manuscript. Also, I'd like to thank my children, Giovanni and Celicia for understanding my late nights at the computer reading and writing.

"Power is not revealed by striking hard or often, but by striking true."

Honoré de Balzac (1799-1850)

Chapter 1

Dominique walked the white- haired, older gentleman past the bar area of the restaurant to the doors leading out to the streets of Washington DC. Holding her hand out, she said, "You take care now. I am glad that we were finally able to get together."

The man took her hand between both of his. "Dominique, the pleasure has been all mine. I am sorry it's taken so long to meet up, and I am glad you had some free time this evening. Ever since Ralph told me of the great job you were doing for him, I have wanted to meet you. I can't believe it's taken two months!"

"Well, better late than never," Dominique laughed. "I hope we can do business together."

"I already know we can. I'll be down at your office on Monday with a substantial portfolio of my investments for you to have a look at and take over their control. I like to think I am a good judge of character, and I think you are a fireball. You're definitely the type of person I want to have manage my portfolio."

"You are too kind, Mr. Morrison. I'm scheduled to be in all day on

Monday. Give me a call in the morning and let me know what time you will be arriving."

"Please, Dominique, call me Rich. I have to get home now, before my wife begins to wonder where I've been."

"Fine, Rich, I'll see you on Monday. Have a great weekend." Dominique gave a wave of her hand as he left the restaurant. Turning around to pick up her black trench coat from the cloakroom, she stopped and looked at the time on her phone. It was too early on a Friday evening to go back to her condo. She decided to call one of her friends to see if anything fun was going on. *I might as well go back in and have another glass of wine while I'm calling,* she thought, as she headed back into the restaurant.

She found a seat at the bar. The bartender noticed her as she walked in, placed a napkin down and asked her what she was having. She ordered a glass of malbec, which she'd recently heard of and wanted to try, and asked the bartender to keep her seat open while she went to the restroom.

Coming out of one of the stalls, she went over to the sink in front of the big mirror to wash her hands. Dominique looked approvingly at the shapely woman looking back at her. Today she had her dark locks of hair tumbling in waves to her shoulders and down her back. Just a shade past thirty years old, her youthful face could pass for someone in college. She was in her best professional suit with a navy blue Armani jacket and skirt. The cream-colored blouse stood out in stark contrast to her brown skin. Though it was undoubtedly business dress, the outfit showed off her voluptuous breasts and ample ass that men seemed to drool over. If she had lived at the time of the Renaissance when Rubens was painting, she would definitely have been one of his models. Her deep caramel complexion was flawless. Her curves were in all the right places, and her hours at the gym kept everything tight and firm. She often snuck peeks in the mirror when she was working out and never failed to spy some guy, whether young or old, admiring her body. She loved teasing the men and women at the gym. She often wondered what went through their minds as they watched her breasts shake and her rounded ass bounce up and down as she ran on the treadmill. It usually gave her a warm glow deep inside. It was nice to be admired and even lusted over. She thought it was too bad that very few of the poor buggers, who gaped at her, could handle her.

She thought back to a of couple hours ago when she had introduced herself to Richard Morrison as she walked over to his table. They had chatted on the phone a few times, but this evening was the first time they had met. He was a nice enough guy who had a lot of money and was looking for someone to better manage some of his financial dealings. This was the business Dominique was in, and she was good at it. For a man who ran a successful company, Morrison had acted like a boy from high school when Dominique firmly shook his hand and told him how happy she was to meet him. His eyes had almost bulged out of his head as he had taken in the woman in front of him. Dominique knew she projected an aura of power and sexuality, which had been intentionally developed and refined over the past ten years. To an unsuspecting man, it was like being sucked into the vortex of a black hole.

To Morrison's credit, his gaze had not focused on her boobs the entire afternoon like some men's. They had talked about his past experiences with folks who worked on his investment portfolio and what he was looking for in the future. He was naturally charmed by Dominique and impressed with her wealth of financial knowledge and ideas. Dominique thought it had been one of her best interviews with a potential client. Maybe it was because she had made the effort to meet him for dinner on a Friday night, since his time was at a premium. It certainly made for a leisurely chance to discuss his financial concerns. It worked out much better than meeting in the confines of someone's office, or watching the clock when talking over lunch.

Dominique left the ladies room smiling and feeling quite content. Having Morrison as a new client would certainly be a feather in her cap at the financial services agency where she worked. Sooner or later, they had to make her a partner at the firm. If they did, it would certainly be on her terms. She had made that clear to her boss.

She went back to her seat at the bar, and wondered what she was going to do for the rest of the night and weekend. She had no plans, but that was fine. Sometimes she enjoyed spontaneity and liked to see what life brought her way. She took her seat and sipped the wine, which wasn't bad at all. She took her phone from her pocketbook and put it in front of her. Dominique thought about which girlfriend to call first, but then let her eyes wander around the room. People watching were one of her favorite pastimes.

Washington DC had many fine restaurants. The Hamilton was one of them. Dominique was pleased when Morrison had suggested it, because she had not been there in quite some time. Looking around the room she saw the usual tables of politicians and powerbrokers, although not as many as during the week perhaps, since it was Friday. However, even in Washington they took a break from their main business of maneuvering their way to whatever power summit interested them. There was a table of military brass in their uniforms enjoying themselves. Couples or groups of people looking for a nice meal and the chance to unwind at the end of the week took up most of the restaurant. When she had first come in a few minutes before, Dominique had noticed that the bar was hopping; it must have been Happy Hour. A few tables around the bar were filled with couples smiling and talking earnestly with each other. *The guys are trying to get pussy,* thought Dominique, *and the women are deciding if they want to give in to them.*

Smiling at her silent joke, Dominique looked around to see who was sitting at the bar with her. To her right were two businessmen who looked like they had been there for too long. They had the red faces and glassy eyes of having had a few drinks too many. To her left, there was another woman sitting at the very end of the bar, two or three seats over from Dominique. She had dark hair and an olive complexion. She looked like she had come directly from some type of office job, based on the slacks and white shirt she was wearing. The woman was talking on a cell phone and suddenly twisted in her chair, giving Dominique the chance to see her face. It was a face that was more girl than woman. She looked very young and wore glasses, with her hair pinned up in a bun. Dominique could hear the girl's end of the conversation on the phone.

"I have been here for two hours waiting for you! And now you tell me you can't make it? You couldn't call or text?" The girl's voice raised in pitch. "You said there was nobody else. What do you mean you ran into an old friend?" She paused as she listened. "Well, fuck you, if I am not enough of a woman for you. Go to hell!" She clicked off and put the phone down. Dominique watched the girl's face start to crumble and tears begin to trickle down behind the glasses.

Dominique's heart was moved by the absolute sadness and hurt emulating from the girl. She gathered up her pocketbook and her wine and was about to move down closer to her, when she felt a hand touching her shoulder. She turned and saw one of the businessmen who had been at the bar. She looked past the man's shoulder and saw his friend eagerly looking on. Turning her attention back to the first one, she barked, "May I help you?"

"Well," he slurred a little, "my friend and I are in town for the weekend. We have a big business deal going on with the Pentagon." He said this last word so pompously that it sounded more like pen-di-gan. "We thought you might want to join us for a little fun tonight."

"Is that right? And why would I be interested in you and your friend?" Dominique coolly asked.

"Because you look like a woman who could handle us both. When we saw you walking around, we figured you would appreciate a couple of real men."

Dominique appraised the man and his partner. "Tell you what. If you two can find a couple of real men, let me know. If I wanted either of you, you would have been the first to know. Because that is the way it works. As for you two fellows, I have other things to do. Enjoy your time in D.C. and have a good evening." Dominique slid off her stool and stood right in front of him, looking him directly in the eyes. She planted the spiky heel of one of her black Jimmy Choo shoes directly into the foot of the fool in front of her. To his credit, he did not cry out. He just winced, but tears formed in his eyes. "Just as I thought, you could never handle me. Now excuse me." She pushed past the inebriated loser, pivoted, and walked over to the girl.

Behind her glasses, the girl's eyes were red and filled with tears but wide-eyed, since she had a front row seat to the little encounter. Dominique handed the girl a tissue, "I am sorry to intrude, but you looked upset. Do you want to go over to that empty table?" She indicated a spot at the edge of the bar area. "You look like you may want to talk and I find the atmosphere at the bar suddenly toxic."

The girl nodded numbly, picked up the remains of her drink, and followed Dominique over to the empty table. Once seated, Dominique introduced herself. "My name is Dominique La Belle. I couldn't help but hear the end of your conversation. I could tell you were hurting."

Sniffling a little, the girl said, "My name's Veronica Cala. I am sorry you saw that. It was so silly."

"Hey, we all have our bad days. I know from experience that

sometimes it helps to talk about stuff. I know you don't know me, but I am a good listener. Two ears and no waiting."

Veronica smiled a little. "Thank you. It was nothing really. It was some guy I had been sort of seeing for a few months. Nothing serious. Tonight was our six-month anniversary and then he stood me up. No big deal…I have been stood up before."

Dominique looked the girl over. If you looked past the glasses and generic business clothes she wore, the young woman was pretty. It did not seem like Veronica's confidence matched her attractiveness, though. Dominique asked, "What do you mean by 'stood up before?' Do you mean by the same man?"

"No, no," said Veronica. "Different men. I guess I don't do well with them. I can never find one that treats me well."

"How do you treat them?" asked Dominique.

"I try to give them what they want. I work at being the attentive girl who wants to please them. It works for a time. Then they either get tired of me or…" Veronica hesitated. Dominique took a sip of her wine and gave her an encouraging look. Veronica sucked in some air and quickly said, "Or the couple of times that I went all the way and had sex with them, they dropped me afterwards." The young woman looked like she was going to cry again.

Dominique fished out a couple more tissues and handed them to the girl. "Here, dry your eyes."

Veronica took off her glasses and wiped her eyes. She blew her nose with a rather loud honk and looked at Dominique ruefully. "Wow, I'm a mess. Let me go wash up. I'll be right back." Veronica got up and hurried to the rest room. Dominique noticed she had a cute figure and a nice wiggle to her walk. She flagged down a waitress, requested another glass of wine, and asked her to find out from the bartender what Veronica was having and bring her a refill.

Dominique decided to talk with the girl for as long as she needed. This was one of those situations that seemed right to Dominique. She thought she could be of help to Veronica. Dominique had developed excellent instincts where people were concerned, and she had a feeling their meeting like this might be good for both of them. If not, then she will have had a nice conversation with someone new and there was nothing wrong with that.

The drinks came at the same time as Veronica returned. She looked a little surprised and said, "Thank you. I was actually going to just head home, but this is nice. I appreciate you coming over to me."

"We all have to deal with men. Depending on what you want, how you treat them can help you to get it," said Dominique.

"I saw how you took care of that jerk at the bar," said Veronica. "I was impressed. I like how he went away with his tail between his legs."

"You liked it, huh?" asked Dominique.

"I thought it was great. I mean, that's what I wish I could do. Deep down inside of me, I want to be able to deal with men like that. Sometimes I think about it. I don't like always being the one giving in. It certainly hasn't gotten me anywhere."

"Well, the good thing is you can't have been dealing with guys for too many years. How old are you?"

"Twenty two," answered Veronica.

"Are you from this area?"

"No, I'm from Edison, New Jersey. I went to school down here at George Washington University. I got an internship at an investment firm during my senior year and they offered me a job when I graduated last May. So I have been on my own down here for almost a year."

"Do you like it?" asked Dominique.

"I don't know," said Veronica. She took a healthy pull at her drink. "The work is interesting but I am treated like the coffee girl at work. I get all of the little shit jobs to do. I share an apartment with two other girls who work in the government and dating has been the pits. The guys I have been attracted to are either gay, married, or assholes." She rolled her eyes. "The one I was talking to on the phone fits into the last category."

Dominique chuckled, "You're going to find a lot of that. Whether it's your job or the relationship you want with a man, it is up to you to decide what you want and then go after it."

"You know, I saw you at the restaurant with that older white guy earlier. Just watching you, I figured you were some kind of top line executive or lobbyist or something like that. What do you do?"

Dominique could see this gal was observant. "I'm in the financial field also. I've been doing it since I was your age. I help people…preferably rich people…manage their money."

"Are you married?"

"No, I am not," said Dominique shaking her head. "It would take a very special man to handle me and get married."

"What do you mean?" asked Veronica.

"Let's just say that when it comes to men, I am in charge. There are a lot of men who like it, but very few can manage it over the long haul because they bore me quickly."

Veronica's eyes were as wide as saucers. "Really! You tell them what you want?"

"Yes. I have always been like that. Now, I have to admit it took me some time to figure myself out and how to best conduct myself. But we are all a work in progress. I am still learning. The bottom line is that I am a Goddess and a man better treat me that way or I don't give him the time of day."

Veronica lowered her voice, "Do you mean in the bedroom too?"

Dominique broke out in a hearty laugh, "Honey, the bedroom, the kitchen, over the desk in his office…whatever. Yes, that is exactly what I mean. And I have to admit, I've also learned to channel this force inside of me into work. Not in a sexual way. But so others know exactly what I want and that it would not be wise for them to go up against me. And when another strong man or woman goes up against me in business, it's fine. I love the challenge. Same for relationships and sex!"

The girl was staring at Dominique with her mouth open. She realized this and reached down for her drink. She took a sip and put the glass down. "I would love to be like you. I know I'm not happy being walked all over wherever I go. It's starting to get old. I know I do not want the rest of my life to be like that. On the other hand, I don't know how to change."

"Veronica, the important thing is that you know you have to change. It didn't happen overnight for me. Now, I admit, I don't think I was ever as unassuming as you, but I ran into a few people over the years who helped me find the person I am. These days, I do not make any apologies for it. I like who I am and there is a lot less stress just being myself, instead of what I think others want me to be."

"Boy, you just summed up where I'm at," said Veronica.

"When you are not bogged down in work or dealing with assholes like the guy from tonight, how do you see yourself?" asked Dominique.

Veronica took her time answering. When she did, it was in a low voice and she started blushing. "I want people to respect me and listen to me. In work, I want to be one of those women that lead people, especially men. They should know that I am a person who knows what I'm doing."

Dominique eyed her, "And what about in a relationship?"

"Lately, I have been picturing myself with a man tied down in front of me and I'm whipping him! That probably has something to do with tonight." She laughed. *Or Maybe I should imagine being tied down and whipped, because I'm so naïve on how to gain power over a man.*

"How are you going to go about it and become that woman?"

The girl looked at Dominique with pleading eyes. "I don't know?"

Dominique looked away for a minute and considered the situation. It was an idea she had thought of before, but never really pursued. This was a good time in her life to do something about it. Dominique was a feminist and truly believed in empowering other women. She wanted to stretch herself more in what she was doing with her dominant nature. She liked this girl. Dominique could tell there was something way down in Veronica aching to come out. They were also in the same industry. She could certainly be helpful to the young woman in that way too. This seemed like such a win-win situation, so why not?

Dominique finally said, "I would very much like to help you. Tell you what, I really want you to think about what we've talked about over the weekend." Dominique pulled out one of her business cards and a pen, and scribbled something on the back. She then checked her calendar on her phone. "That's my card with my personal cell number on the back. If you really want to learn how to empower yourself at work and with men, give me a call by Sunday night. I am free Thursday evening after work, and if you are available, we can get together for a drink." I know this great spot that has an excellent happy hour and lots of eye candy. We can meet at the Nightclub/Restaurant, Park at 14th.

"Dominique, thank you very much. I will think it over, but I know I'm going to say yes." Veronica blushed again, "Yes, I cannot wait to get started. I'll become your Goddess protégé."

Chapter 2

$\mathcal{D}$ominique walked through to the bar where she was to meet

Veronica. A last minute call with a client had delayed her. She hoped that

the young woman had waited. She liked Veronica. It was also very

appealing that the girl looked to her as her mentor. Dominique felt ready to

fill this role. After all, what could be better than helping another woman

realize her potential? Maybe her experiences would help Veronica avoid

some of the pitfalls that she herself had encountered.

Looking around the bar, Dominique couldn't see the young girl. The

club was crowded, the music was low and the roar of the people talking

provided a nice background. The Park at 14th was Dominique's favorite

happy hour place on Thursdays. She had reserved the table and the waiters

would take good care of her. When she got to the back of the club, she

would see that a bottle of her favorite chardonnay would be on the table in

a bucket of ice. Then she saw a hand waving at her. Veronica was wearing her hair down and Dominique noticed that it was long, wavy and beautiful. She was wearing a two-piece navy suit with a white blouse and had a big smile on her face. As Dominique got closer, she saw that the suit was typical bank-teller attire.

Dominique knew that she looked good today. She was wearing a black pencil skirt that went a tad past her thigh and a matching jacket. Under the jacket, she sported a blood red, silk shirt that coordinated nicely with her nails. With the top few buttons undone, she was aware of the cleavage she displayed. Out of the corner of her eye, Dominique saw that the guy who had just tripped over his chair had also noticed. She smiled at this and sat down across from Veronica.

"I am so sorry I'm late. One of my bigger customers called me as I was heading out the door. With some of these people, you have to hold their hand all the time. He needed some of my TLC, so I couldn't leave quite when I'd planned. Did my assistant, Jaron, call you to let you know I'd be a few minutes late?"

"Yes, he did. No worries, I understand. The table is nice and your waiters Chase and Andre have been taking good care of me. I've been drinking my wine, and watching the comings and goings of the people here," said Veronica.

Andre, the waiter, was sexy, young and tall, with hazel eyes and a very nice build. He came over and interrupted them. "Dominique, I have your chilled glass waiting for you. I will be right back with it." Veronica indicated that she was ready for a refill. Andre disappeared and quickly returned with another glass. He poured Veronica a second glass of wine as the two women chatted about their respective workdays. Dominique remembered what it was like starting out in the finance industry, as Veronica explained some of the things she was going through at her workplace.

An attractive man walked by, interrupted and said to Dominique,

"Your shoes are very sexy. Can I buy you ladies a drink?" Dominique thanked him for the compliment but said that they still had a half a bottle of wine. He replied that he would love them to take him up on his offer of a drink and gave Dominique his business card. Dominique smiled and watched him walk away.

"Dominique, you make it look so easy. You are so confident," Veronica said.

Dominique looked at the business card. "He's looking for a strong woman and he has a foot fetish."

"A foot fetish? You could pick that up from a ten second conversation?"

"Yes, did you see the way he looked at my shoes? I have my blouse open and cleavage showing and he only glanced at it. It was the tone in his voice when he said that he liked my shoes, as if he wanted to massage my feet. But we're here to talk about you. Are you feeling better than you did last week?"

Veronica blushed, "I was so upset with myself that I let myself get like that over a guy. I don't ever want to be like that again." She smiled, "I want to be like you!"

Dominique laughed, "It's important for you to just be yourself. However, I do know that sometimes we need some encouragement to bring who we really are to the surface. You have to remember; the person you see here has been a work in progress. Ten years ago, I hadn't tapped into everything I was going to be. I had a good idea of what I wanted in a relationship with a man, work and life, but was having trouble releasing what I call the 'Goddess' inside of me."

"How did you go about it?" Veronica asked seriously.

"It was a combination of things. I knew from the time I was a young girl that I had this dominant streak in me. I had a couple of relationships where I tried to bring it out with the guys I was with. Then about eight years ago, I met an Australian. He held the key that unlocked everything inside of me. After that, it was a combination of research and trying different things, as I explored my desires and boundaries."

"How did he do that?" asked Veronica. "Tell me more about this Australian. What do you mean 'he held the key?'"

"It was one of those times where another person saw me clearly for the person I am. Let me tell you how we met."

"Sure," said Veronica. "I have been looking forward all day to talking with you. I want to hear everything you have to say."

Dominique said, "Okay. Let me tell the story and then you can ask any questions you may have. Agreed?"

Veronica nodded her assent. Dominique took a sip of wine and launched into her tale.

****

I burst through the door into the cold, Washington DC sunshine. It was lunchtime and I already felt like I'd put in a full day at the financial services firm where I worked. In an office of 32 financial advisers, there were only four women holding those key positions. I was one of them and the only black woman. In fact, there were only two African-Americans on the entire senior staff. While there was a sense of competition within the office, we all got along fairly well. Still, after dealing with a particularly troublesome client for most of the morning, I decided to go out for lunch and take a break before starting on my afternoon work.

I remember taking a quick glance at my reflection in the large, plate glass window that fronted my office building. I thought I looked good. My smile was bright, and I had to nod in approval at how I looked in my winter coat. It kept me warm, but still managed to show off my figure. "Damn," I said aloud, "I didn't think I could find something like this that would cover me up, keep me warm and still show my curves." I started walking down the block.

As I walked to the corner and waited for a light to change, I heard a deep, sexy voice behind me say, "Nice ass." I looked behind me and saw a tall, solidly built man smiling at me. His faced was tanned and rugged-looking, and he appeared very strong by the way he filled out his jacket. I scanned the rest of the crowd at the corner to see who the comment was aimed at. Then I noticed the Australian accent as he said, "I'm talking to you!"

I quickly shot back, "You cannot be talking to me. Not like that." I realized I wouldn't have responded at all if it were not for the guy's own smile and the Down Under accent. He would not have been the first man, and certainly won't be the last, that I would just walk away from and leave in the proverbial dust.

I took a closer look at the man, and saw that the black, woolen beanie he was wearing left a few brown curls peeking out from the back. The black jacket he wore was unzipped, revealing the definition of his body and a powerful chest underneath a navy blue turtleneck. He was very muscular and his entire demeanor was one of authority and strength. To many others he would have been an intimidating presence, but not to me. I just found the Aussie intriguing.   He came up to me and introduced himself as Xavier Adams. He lived in a suburb on the outskirts of Melbourne, Australia and this was his first visit to Washington DC. He beamed his smile at me and said, "This may be very forward of me, but would you care to accompany me to lunch?"

I gave him a cool, appraising glance for a moment then I looked directly into his bright, green eyes and asked, "Are all the men in Australia as shy as you?"

He chuckled at my sarcasm. "We have our share of quiet blokes, but I never saw much use in it. I live my life with the motto, nothing ventured, and nothing gained. The worse you could say is 'no' and I would go eat by myself. Of course, I'd be heartbroken if I lost my chance to talk with the sexiest woman I have run into since getting to this lovely city."

I did admire his confidence. "Tell you what we can do. I'm heading over to Chop't to get a salad, but I don't have a lot of time. I have things to get done at work this afternoon. And my name is Dominique."

He offered me his arm. "Love the name. Lead on then. I'll take whatever time I can get with you."

I linked arms with him and strolled to one of my favorite lunch spots. It was only a block away from where he had complimented my ass. Once again, I sent out kudos to my coat for not hiding my assets. As we entered the restaurant, I noticed how people looked at us as he held the door open for me. In fact, I observed on our short walk together that others got out of his way when they saw us coming. I liked that. I didn't have room or time in my life for men that weren't alpha males with a commanding presence.

We placed our order and found a table. Xavier and I chatted about Washington and the sites he had seen so far. Our salads came, and after a couple of bites, Xavier looked directly in my eyes and said, "I was walking by when you exploded out of the door of your office building. I have to say that I was taken aback. My first impression was that you were someone who is sexy, strong, and sensual. When we started talking, I could also tell you are highly intelligent. Do you know what a unique combination that is in today's world?"

I finished chewing and looked at him keenly, "How do I know you don't say that to every woman you meet? It sounds like a line."

"Listen, Dominique," Xavier continued earnestly, "I work out in the middle of the ocean on an oil rig. It's not an easy life, though it has its perks. I make good money. We work for a month, and then we get a month off. I love to travel and that is what I do during most of my off months. I have visited many different countries and met many different women on my journeys. I can honestly say that from my experience you are exceptionally beautiful and I would love to get to know you better."

I raised a questioning brow and purred with a voice loaded with honey, "And just how would you like to get to know me, Xavier?"

He continued to look into my eyes, "Dominique, I want to take care of your every need. I would love to devote my life to pleasing you."

I quietly looked at Xavier as I lifted a forkful of salad to my mouth. I chewed on it as my thoughts went racing. I remember thinking, *Wow, I have heard some outrageous pick-up lines before, but this dude is pouring it on heavy. He just met me! A guy will say anything just to get some pussy.* But while I was thinking this, I realized that my bullshit detector was not picking up any bad vibes. I could read his body language and sense that he was getting excited. I could tell by the tone of his voice, the way he was breathing, the shine in his eyes, and his twitching pecks that the dude seemed sincere. I found him really attractive and could feel the chemistry between us. Even I was breathing a bit faster, had a dry mouth and moisture between my legs. I decided to put Xavier to the test to see if he meant what he said. I looked directly into his eyes and said, "You can show me better than you can tell me, Xavier."

Xavier reached across the table and took my hand. He brought it up to his lips and softly kissed it. Still holding me, he said in a tone of longing and sincerity, 'I would love to show you.'

I took my hand away and said, "Settle down, big boy. Good things come to those who wait. Let's finish lunch because I do have to get back to my office."

We moved on from the intense moment and went back to small talk about our respective occupations. Once lunch was done, Xavier escorted me back to my office building. Standing outside, we exchanged cell phone numbers. I extended my hand and he grasped it with both of his. Once more, he said, "Dominique, I meant what I said. I will make you very happy."

I gave him a big smile and a half-hearted eye roll and thanked him for lunch. I wished him well in Washington and hurried inside to get out of the cold. Walking over to the elevator, I thought a little more about Xavier. As a man, he greatly appealed to me. He was good-looking and easy to talk with. He had that aura of power about him. That is what appealed to me the most. But unlike many women, I don't give in to a man's power. I loved to turn that around and have the man give in to me!

I got out of the elevator and strolled to my office, saying hello to colleagues and staff that I saw along the way. Going through my door, I automatically looked out the large window that's behind my desk. Ten stories above the street afford me a great view of the Potomac River. I never get tired of looking at it. On that day, I could look across the river into Northern Virginia and see the bright sunlight bathing the scenery in a beautiful glow. Even with the leafless trees, the view allowed my mind to relax no matter what else was going on.

I hung my coat up behind the door and wrestled to get my mind into work mode. Sitting down at my computer, my eyes skimmed over what the stock market was doing. The figures showed a good day, with the Dow, S&P and NASDAQ going up by midafternoon. I believe that I am a woman of many talents and strengths, and one of them is the ability to focus intently on my job. After all, when I make my clients money, I make money. And when you cater to a clientele with an average net worth of $25 million, you are not talking about loose change.

I briefly wondered if I'd caused anything to go 'up' for Xavier during our encounter. I thought about the slight bulge in his pants when he'd stood up from lunch and wondered about the size. I thought about the way he grabbed my hand and his soft touch. I also thought about the things I wanted to do to him and how I would love to get my hands on him. I imagined how nice it would be to kiss his lips from the way he touched and caressed my hand, and how it would feel for him to taste me.

After several minutes, I shook the notion right out of my head and got totally into my work. But then the texts from Xavier started coming around two thirty in the afternoon. I answered them when I could. In the beginning I smiled at the messages. They were all about how Xavier wanted to please me and make me happy. He told me of his commitment to my desires. Finally, he texted, "Making you happy will make me the happiest man on earth!"

This was the point when I decided it was all complete bullshit! If I had to hear one more time how Xavier just wanted to live to please me, I would smash my phone against the wall. He just wanted some pussy! Besides, exchanging texts like this was boring, and I was much too busy to waste time on something that was not going to lead anywhere. With that thought, I stopped responding to his texts and did not answer when he tried to call.

After a few days of nonstop work, I found myself home at my condominium. I flipped through the television channels, puttered around in the kitchen, and found myself totally bored. I love my work, but it is not how I define myself. Work is a means to an end. I always look at myself as the total embodiment of a powerful and sensual woman. Like the goddess of love and beauty, Aphrodite, the Pharaoh Cleopatra used her beauty to her advantage and seduced Julius Caesar to keep her on her throne. The beautiful Freya, goddess of love, beauty, fertility and magic, was the goddess of sensual love. And Isis was the queen of all goddesses. I have always thought that ancient cultures would've look upon me as a Goddess. I smiled at this thought. *Hell, there is no reason these minion males of the 21st century can't think of me the same way! Chivalry is not dead!*

I was still chuckling as I saw my reflection in the mirror hanging on the wall in the hallway. I had stripped down to a sports bra and panties. As I glanced down at my butt, I remembered how Xavier had called out to me the other day. *Wow*, I thought, *if he liked my ass in that coat, he wouldn't be able to contain himself now if he was here!*

With that thought, I shook off my feelings of boredom, went into the kitchen and picked up my cell phone from the counter. I saw that Xavier had texted a couple of times and had tried to call me that afternoon. The texts were the same stuff about serving me to the fullest. Out loud to myself I said, "He has no idea what it means to serve me. Still, he gets marks for persistence…or for being an ungodly pain in the ass." I then pressed Xavier's number to call him back.

The phone had barely rung when I heard in my ear, "Hello. I'm so glad you called." The breathlessness and excitement in his voice sounded like one of my nephews on Christmas morning.

"Hi there, Xavier. I'm sorry I've been out of touch the past few days. I've been busy."

"That's quite okay. I was afraid you didn't want to talk to me anymore."

"Oh, Xavier, you shouldn't think that. If I was easy, it wouldn't be any fun."

"I know you are very busy, Dominique. And you probably have more men knocking at your door than there are pubs in Melbourne. But I want you to know that I really mean what I've been texting you. Since we met, I can only think of doing whatever it takes to make you the happiest woman in the world. I guess I am asking for a chance to do just that."

"Well, Xavier, the jury is still out on how sincere you are with all of this. As I told you at lunch, show me!"

"Then let me take you out to dinner. Tomorrow is Friday. Do you have any plans after work?"

"I was going to get together with a couple of my girls, but we have an understanding that things may come up to change those plans. I think for this, I can make myself available."

"What time do you finish work?"

"I try to get out of there by six on Fridays."

"Then I will pick you up at your office at six."

With that, I ended the call, sat down on my sofa and stretched. I smiled as I said to the room, "I guess I'll see if Mr. Xavier has what it takes to please me or not."

The next evening, I locked my office door and headed to the elevator with my coat draped over my arm. In my peripheral vision, I noticed that the few men and women left in the office followed me with their eyes. I was wearing a silky, black dress that wafted around me like a mist. The front draped my chest to highlight my ample cleavage and big breasts and the rest showed off my round ass and incredibly toned legs. I knew that I looked good. I had also put up with the stares and comments all day at the office. Although I was always well dressed at work, today I had definitely raised the bar. I was actually looking forward to Xavier's reaction to my outfit. I wanted it to get a rise out of him at first glance.

The elevator slowed to a halt and the doors opened to let me out. I put on my coat and exited the building. I expected to see Xavier waiting at the door, but there was no sign of him. I did notice a black, Lincoln Town Car at the curb, but no Xavier. I could not believe it. After all that pursuit, the guy was going to stand me up! I put a check on my anger and began to walk away, wondering if I could still hook up with my friends. I only went about four steps when the door of the Town Car sprang open. The driver raced around the nose of the car and asked, "Are you Dominique?"

I was slightly surprised but said, "Yes, I am."

"Xavier Adams sent me to pick you up and take you to the restaurant."

I hesitated for a moment. I was a bit apprehensive about getting in the car with a driver I did not know to meet a man I barely knew. On the other hand, it was a very nice car and showed a touch of class. I took a deep breath and allowed the driver to guide me into the back of the automobile. As I settled into the seat, I saw a dozen roses laid out next to me accompanied by a black box, wrapped with purple ribbon, and topped with a big bow.

Smiling in delight, I plucked the card that I saw inserted under the ribbon. Opening the envelope, I read, "I thought of you when I saw these. I hope you don't mind." Intrigued, I unwrapped the package and opened the box to see a sexy pair of black, Gucci, strapped sandals nestled in the tissue paper. I gasped aloud. At that time in my life, I had never owned a pair of Gucci shoes, or any expensive heels for that matter. I had to admit, Xavier impressed me.

Even though it was the middle of February, I decided to put the sandals on. Maneuvering around in the back seat, I kicked off my shoes and strapped the new ones on. They felt like silk wrapped around my feet. At that moment, the car pulled up to the 701 Restaurant on Pennsylvania Avenue, one of Washington's more elegant eateries. The driver leapt out and came around to open my door. He offered his hand to help me out of the car. I asked him if he was going to be waiting while we ate. He said he was and that it was perfectly fine to keep the flowers and my other shoes in the car.

I thanked him and headed to the restaurant's door. My feet truly felt like they were walking on clouds. The maître de welcomed me as I walked into the greeting area. When I told him my name, the tuxedo-clad, older gentleman invited me to follow him and glided over to a booth on the quiet side of the dining area, where Xavier had been waiting for me.

Xavier stood up as I approached the table. I instantly noticed that he was stylishly dressed in a dark-blue suit, a white shirt with light-red pinstripe, and a red tie matched by a pocket-handkerchief. I thought, *he may work on an oilrig, but he does know how to dress.* I offered him my hand, which he took in his two, big paws and brought it gently up to his soft lips. He was looking over his hands into my eyes, and I saw the beginnings of a wide smile. He gestured for me to take a seat, but I said, "If you would excuse me for a moment, I'd like to go freshen up first. Then we can relax and enjoy ourselves."

Xavier gave an almost courtly bow as I headed to the rest room. My mind was racing. *What is this guy up to? How did he know my shoe size? This is one of the nicest and most expensive places in town. On top of that, he sent a car and driver. I don't know what his motives are, but girl, I think I am just going to enjoy this and ride it out to see what happens.* When I'd finished freshening up, I took a deep breath and headed back to the table.

Xavier had a huge smile on his face as he watched me walking towards him. He greeted me with, "You are truly beautiful tonight. I'm so happy that you are wearing the shoes. Do you like them?"

I sat down and looked at my feet. "They are gorgeous. My feet feel like they died and went to heaven."

Xavier touched my chin with his finger and lifted my head. "Dominique, I want you to enjoy yourself tonight. All I ask is that you just be yourself, and give me a chance." He said it with so much sincerity, that the last of my doubts faded away. He ordered a bottle of the most expensive champagne on the menu.

We began talking like old friends who had known each other for years. Xavier told me about how he worked as an engineer on the oilrigs and that the company had recently promoted him. During his month of duty, he was the overall boss of the rig. Then he described some of the beautiful places around the world he had traveled to when he was off duty, and talked about the ones he still had to visit.

It was when he was talking about his travels that Xavier said, "Even with everywhere I've been, I have to say that you are the most beautiful woman I have ever seen!"

This comment got my attention. I got that skeptical feeling back that I had when reading his texts. I got very serious and leaned a little closer to Xavier. "I cannot figure you out. You obviously did a lot of planning for this evening, but what is your deal? What are you up to?"

Xavier smiled and said, "I mean it. I just want to please you." He kept looking into my eyes and after a moment said, "Nothing would please me more than to rub your beautiful feet."

I decided to call his bluff and see if this guy was for real or not. "In that case, you can rub them right now." And with that I lifted both feet onto his lap.

I wondered for a second if he would back down. Instead, his smile got wider as he slowly unbuckled my sandals one by one. My eyes got larger as he began to massage my feet right there at the table. His touch seemed to journey up my leg and I slowly began to feel the moist beginnings of arousal. Here we were in a beautiful public restaurant at a linen covered table and he wanted to sensually massage my feet. I was not the only one feeling the effects. With my feet in his lap, I could feel his cock getting hard. This only turned me on more.

The waiter returned and Xavier continued to rub my feet in front of him with one hand while producing a hundred dollar bill out of his pocket with the other, which he gave to the waiter. He also gave him our dinner order, and thanked him for his excellent service. The waiter walked away as if he hadn't seen anything. I tried to take my feet away from Xavier, but he quickly grabbed them and said, "We don't want your precious feet touching this dirty floor." He then took his time putting my new sandals back on.

The waiter came back again to refill our champagne glasses, looked at me, and smiled. This began to make me feel a little uncomfortable, so I decided it was time to take control. I looked Xavier in the eyes and asked, "What are your intentions?"

He smiled back at me, leaned over, and said, "Dominique, I know you are a strong woman that is very demanding, confident, knows what she wants, and is not afraid to tell a man exactly how to treat her. I know you enjoy telling men what to do."

I admired his perception. I said, "Yes, I can be very bossy at times, but I am trying to work on it. I know it is not easy to love a woman like me. I am very hard to please."

Xavier grabbed my hand. Shaking his head, he said, "No, those are the qualities that I look for in a woman. And I do not want you to change anything about you. I think you are flawless. That is why I told you that you are the perfect woman for me. You are exactly what I've been looking for."

It did not happen often, but I was speechless. All my life, other people had told me that a woman should be submissive to a man. It was important that a woman should be this dainty little girl and let the man be the ruler. Growing up, I watched my mother play down her intelligence just to make my father feel more like a man. For years, I never saw my mother challenge my father. He made all the family decisions, even if my mother knew they were wrong and she disagreed with him.

Now, finally, a man that appreciated a strong, sexy and intelligent woman was here with me. In past relationships or encounters, I had made forays into being domineering over a man, but they had never been received well. Here was a handsome and accomplished guy, practically begging me to take control. I decided this was not an opportunity I was going to let slip away from me.

We throttled back the sensual tension a bit as we ate dinner. The conversation was enjoyable as we chatted about everything from sports to politics. The time seemed to fly by as we enjoyed the delicious food and each other's company. Once dinner was over and we got up to leave, Xavier did something that truly astounded me. He got down on his hands and knees and kissed my toes! I immediately felt an electric shock deep in my pussy, but quickly slapped Xavier on the back of his head and told him to get up. He smiled as if what he did was an everyday occurrence, and helped me into my coat.

I slowly shook my head at Xavier's display, but I also knew I was going to have him come home with me. We left the restaurant as the Town Car promptly zipped to a stop in front of us. Xavier held the door open for me and I settled into the seat. He went around to the other side, carefully moved the roses and sat down. Xavier's foot massage in the restaurant had been such a turn on that I immediately took control. I pushed him back into the seat, pulled my dress up, straddled him and started kissing him hard and passionately. I started at his ear, biting on the ear lobe and then circling my tongue around his ear. Then I kissed slowly down the side of his neck and met him on his lips. There was so much passion in our kiss. My fingers raked his hair as I pressed my breasts into him. The way that his big strong hands grabbed my waist sent chills all over my body. We were getting so into it that I didn't think we would make it to the condo.

When we got to my place and I got out of the car, I saw that I had left a wet spot on his trousers. Xavier had a difficult time getting out of the car and quickly tried to adjust himself so that the huge bulge in his pants wouldn't show. He tried to nonchalantly thank the driver as he gathered up the flowers and the shoebox holding my old shoes.

When we entered the building, we headed to the elevator. I knew the other people around us could sense the sexual tension between us. When we got to my floor, I grabbed him by the arm and led him to my condo. As soon as we were inside, I pressed him up against the wall and kissed him some more. Xavier pulled back and said, "Please let me enjoy this moment." He dumped the flowers and box on a nearby table, and dropped to his knees. Kneeling before me he said, "I want to be yours, Dominique. I want to be a love slave to you. I want you to be my Goddess. Please be my Goddess, Dominique." Then he bent over and kissed my toes. "Let me worship your beautiful toes, my Goddess. He slid his tongue up my leg and said, "Let me worship your beautiful legs, my Goddess. He crawled around behind me and kissed my plump ass, saying, "Let me worship your beautiful ass, my Goddess." He crawled back in front me, slowly lifted my dress and tried to kiss my pussy. I placed one hand across his mouth and with the other, pulled my dress back down. "You haven't earned that." Xavier nodded and resumed his kneeling position, looking up like an admonished puppy.

This was the hottest thing I could ever imagine. Wasn't it just the night before that I thought of myself as a Goddess? I was so turned on. I had experienced this before, but only after having sex. Never did a man come so willingly and openly to please me. I could feel the moisture building up between my legs and a flow of sweet juices start to trickle down them.

Trying to subdue my excitement, I walked away from Xavier and took a seat on the couch. He followed me on his hands and knees, crawling like an animal. He stayed in that position as he said, "I know that I am taller than you, but I want to show you that I want to be submissive to you." He then came and kneeled before me, placing my heels on his thigh. He picked up my right foot, and began to suck my toes through my stockings. At the same time, he unstrapped my sandals with his other hand and slowly took off my shoes.

I immediately felt a rush. It felt like a heat wave had exploded throughout my body as I cried out, "Oh, my God, I just came." I grabbed Xavier by the hair and pulled his head up.

As we looked at each other, he asked, "What's wrong, my Goddess?"

I felt like I was losing control and had to turn the tables quickly. I told Xavier to get undressed. He stood up without taking his eyes off me and began to unbutton his shirt. It fell to the floor and he stood there bare-chested, displaying his muscles to me. He reached for his pants and I stopped him. "It's my turn now," I said. I began to unbutton his pants and pulled the zipper down. Then I slowly pulled them the rest of the way off. I sat up on the couch and Xavier's cock was staring straight at me through the sexy boxer shorts he was wearing. He had strong muscular thighs and his underwear could barely contain his huge, thickened cock.

I wasn't expecting such girth and I could not wait to touch it. I ached to feel it inside of me. When Xavier kneeled back down in front of me, I demanded, "Undress me!"

He slowly lifted my dress above my hips. He grabbed my pantyhose with his teeth, at the side of my hip, and slowly began to pull them down. As Xavier eased my pantyhose off I began to squirm and roll from side to side to assist him. With all the movement, I accidentally also stepped on his thick, hard cock. Before I could apologize, Xavier let out a roar of pain and screamed, "Yes, Goddess!"

I thought, *Wow, he likes this!*

He finished pulling off my stockings that were saturated with my cum, picked them up in his hands and inhaled a deep breath; as if it was the sweetest rose he had ever smelled. I didn't understand why he smelled my pantyhose, but he sure seemed to like it. As he continued to inhale the scent from them without permission, I walked over and stepped on his cock again. Xavier immediately crumbled and fell to the floor. He resumed kissing my feet saying, "Thank you, Goddess. You know exactly what to do to me!" With tears in his eyes from the pain, he looked up and said, "I knew you were the perfect Goddess for me."

I saw how much pleasure he received from the pain that I inflicted on his cock. I grabbed it and instinctively placed his cock between my feet and began to stroke his thick, hard member with them. Xavier melted and I could see the pleasure in his eyes. He kept repeating, "Yes, Goddess. More, Goddess, please, Goddess."

It got to the point where I was so sick of hearing him barking orders, that I grabbed him by his hair, pulled his head back and yelled in his face, "Shut up and make ME cum!"

Xavier picked me up and carried me to the bedroom. Gently, he laid me on the bed and opened up my legs. He was amazed at how wet and creamy it was around my inner thighs. He slowly kissed me between them, careful not to touch my hot, wet pussy. I was so excited and horny that I couldn't wait any longer. I commanded him to lie down. I rolled over on top of him, and sat on his face. My ass completely smothered his head with my pussy directly on his mouth. Finally, it felt so good with his tongue thrusting deep into my pussy that I had orgasm after orgasm. My cum was drenching Xavier's face. I began to squeeze his head between my legs and every time I felt another surge in my pussy. After riding his face for a few minutes, I felt him squirming and gasping for air from the lack of oxygen. He wouldn't stop, even though I was smothering him with my wet pussy and my ass covering his face. I told him that I would let him go once he made me cum five times in a row. Then I squeezed his head even tighter until I orgasmed for the fifth and sixth time.

After my legs stopped shaking and I relaxed a little, I allowed him to come up for air. He wiped my juices off his face with his hand and took a deep breath. He leaned closer to me and asked if he could please me more. I knew what he wanted, but I wanted to hear him beg. So I asked, "In what way?"

"Please, Goddess Dominique, I want to feel you. Please let me pleasure you."

I asked, "How would you do that, Xavier?"

"Oh, Goddess, I can show you better than just telling you."

I smiled. I knew what he wanted to do and I wanted him to do it as well. At this point, I certainly could not let on that I probably wanted him more then he wanted me. I had to stay in control. I hopped off the bed and told him to lie back down. He did so and enthusiastically said, "Yes, Goddess." He had a look of lust in his eyes. I finished undressing, slowly unbuttoning and then lifting the dress over my head.

Xavier was so excited that he lunged at me like a starving wolf ready to eat fresh flesh. I pushed him down and whispered in his ear, "Relax. I am in control and if you want to continue, you better remember that!"

Xavier said, "Goddess, your body is so beautiful. I have never seen breasts like yours before. They are so big and your nipples are perfect for sucking. I just want to feel them and suck them. Please let me touch them. I will do anything for you."

I looked him in the eye and said, "Anything?"

Xavier said, "Yes, Goddess".

I then told him, "I will let you touch them, but not until I tell you to." With those words, I lie down on the bed. Then I told Xavier to kiss me.

He leaned over, careful not to press his chest up against my breasts. He started to breathe heavily and I felt his hard cock poke me. I grabbed his big, hard penis and pushed its tip right at the center of my pussy. I was so wet that milky white cum dripped onto the bed. When he felt the moisture, his eyes lit up and he asked, "Please, Goddess, can I?"

"Can you what, Xavier?"

"Can I feel you?" He stared at my breasts, fighting the urge to suck them, to touch them.

I was so far past being turned on, but I still wanted to see how far I could push him. Could he really be an obedient love slave and not thrust his huge erection into my hot wet pussy? Here I was, completely naked on my back with his chest so close to my breasts that I could feel the heat. I couldn't see his cock, but I could certainly feel the thick head touching me. All he would have to do is move his hips and in one thrust he would be inside of me.

Xavier was breathing hard and sweat began to roll off his head. He practiced amazing restraint by staying balanced above me without penetrating my pussy. His willpower impressed me, and I was finally ready to feel him inside of me after the last thirty minutes of holding himself above me. I was finished torturing him and myself. I leaned up, grabbed his rock hard cock, and whispered into his ear, "Are you ready?" Without waiting for an answer, I raised my hips up to help guide his engorged dick into my throbbing pink lips. He pushed his hips up against mine. I knew his cock was big, but had no idea just how it would fill me up inside. He pushed and pushed against my tight pussy, trying to force it in.

Xavier looked into my eyes with concern as he was having trouble penetrating me. I was too tight, and he was too big, even with all the cum between my legs that acted as natural lubrication. His cock might actually be too big. He leaned over and whispered, "I will stop if I'm hurting you. I do not want to hurt you, Goddess."

I looked him in the eyes and wrapped my legs around his hips. I reached my arms out to grab his ass and pulled him closer. I said, "Did I tell you to stop?" I rocked my hips back and forth on him. "You stop when I tell you to." I only felt pleasure, not pain, as he slowly pumped his hips. I could feel his thick cock slowly inch deeper and deeper into my opening. Finally, his entire cock was inside me. I could feel it jerking and twitching and I knew he was ready to cum.

I squeezed my body tight to prevent Xavier from moving and said, "You only cum when I tell you to cum."

Xavier gasped, "Goddess, it is so hard not to cum. You feel amazing! I can't help myself, Goddess."

Before I knew it, Xavier pulled out and shot large amounts of sperm over my body. I looked like a vanilla milkshake had spilled on my tits and stomach. He ran into the bathroom to get some wet, hot towels and came back to clean me off. He then sheepishly went into the kitchen and got me a glass of ice water.

We stayed up the remainder of the night laughing and joking. At some point, I fell asleep in Xavier's arms. I woke up early in the morning and saw that Xavier was at the bottom of my bed curled up at my feet.

****

Dominique stopped her story for a second as Andre poured another glass of wine. She took a long drink to soothe her mouth. Veronica was looking at her with her mouth hanging open. Her face was flush and her eyes wide.

Veronica let out a deep breath. "Wow!" was all she said. She took another deep breath and reached out for her wine. Drinking, she tried to bring herself under control. "I think I almost came as I was envisioning what you were saying. That has never happened before!"

Dominique said, "It's amazing what can get us hot. To be honest, reliving that time has me a little worked up too." They both laughed.

Veronica slowly stood. She straightened her dress and said, "Would you excuse me a moment? I have to hit the lady's room. But I want you to tell me everything else that happened with you and Xavier."

"No problem, dear. I am going to ask for some ice water while you are gone. It makes the talking a little easier."

Veronica said, "Please get one for me too. Actually, I could use a bathtub of ice water right now." With that, Veronica started to walk away towards the restrooms. Dominique smiled in amusement, as the girl's legs seemed a little wobbly. "Wait until she hears the rest!" she thought.

The drinks came as Veronica came back to the table and sat down. She still looked a little out of sorts as she took her glasses off. "I just did something I never did before," she whispered breathlessly.

"What's that?" Dominique asked.

"I went into one of the stalls and played with my clit till I came. It certainly didn't take long since you had me so fricking turned on. I had to stick my other hand in my mouth so I didn't yell out. I can be a bit, uh, loud when I cum."

Dominique noted with amusement that Veronica looked both a little embarrassed and relieved at the same time. "Don't worry about it, honey. I think I would be worried about you if you didn't get turned on."

"I think what is really getting to me," said Veronica, "is that this is all real. I can picture you doing everything you did. And you know what?" Her eyes shone. "I want to be able to do all of that too. To have all that control over a man and his cock! And have him *wanting* to please me. Wow!" Dominique checked her phone and said, "It's getting a little late for a workday. How about we meet up again on Saturday morning for brunch and I could tell you more."

"Definitely," said the young woman with unbridled enthusiasm.

"There is this great restaurant in Georgetown called Sequoia's that has an amazing brunch on the weekend. We could meet there around noon."

"Sure, that would be great."

Dominique summoned Andre back to the table, paid the check and they both left the club.

Chapter 3

$\mathcal{D}$ominique arrived at Sequoia's ten minutes early. She was surprised
to see Veronica already sitting at the bench near the front door.

The women embraced and gave each other a kiss on the cheek.

" Dominique, thank you for taking time out of your busy schedule to
meet again."

"It's a pleasure Veronica. It's just nice to be around another beautiful
positive woman."

"Thanks, but I don't consider myself to be beautiful or positive."

"There is always something positive in everything. Just think, I would
never have met you if it were not for your ex-boyfriend standing you up at
the Hamilton. I'm sad that happened to you but I've made a new friend."

They walked into the restaurant and the hostess escorted them to a
table outside, overlooking the Potomac River. The waiter came up and took
their orders. It was a beautiful summer day and the view was incredible.

Veronica eagerly opened up the conversation, "I've been so anxious to hear more about Xavier."

Dominique laughed and said, "Great, because I am eager to tell you more."

****

So, Xavier was curled up at the bottom of my bed when I woke up in the dark hours of the early morning, I had to smile at the sight of him wrapped around my feet as if he was my pet. Nature called and I carefully disentangled my feet from the sleeping man and eased out of bed. I made my way to the bathroom and, just as cautiously, slipped back into bed. I placed my feet back near Xavier so that he could easily find them when he awoke. I started to relive the past evening's activities in my mind, but quickly dropped off to sleep.

The next time I woke up, sunlight was sneaking in through the gaps of the curtains. As I slowly came around, my senses keyed on two things. One, there was an incredibly pleasant smell of food wafting its way into the bedroom. The second sensation was that my pussy ached. It didn't hurt, it was more like the feeling my body gets after a great session at the gym. *Well, yes,* I thought, *I guess you could call last night one heck of a workout. If I could sell it as an exercise video, I'd be a millionaire.*

I made my way out of the bedroom and headed to the bathroom. I splashed water on my face, brushed my teeth, put lip gloss on my lips, ran a brush through my hair and put on the white, silk robe I had hanging on the back of the door. I took a quick look in the mirror. I did not look like I performed in the sex Olympics last night. In fact, I looked quite refreshed and I liked the twinkle in my eyes. With that, I tip toed out of the bathroom into the kitchen to see what Xavier was doing.

I stopped in surprise as I got to the living room. Xavier was walking around in his sexy boxer shorts dusting the furniture. Off to the side, I saw my vacuum cleaner standing at attention and ready to be used. The roses from last night were in a vase sitting on an end table. Astonishingly, it looked like there were two-dozen more fresh roses sitting on the coffee table- "Thank God," I said to myself, "that I am not allergic to flowers."

Xavier became aware of my presence. "Good day, Goddess," he said as his wide smile brightened his face. "I trust that you slept well?"

"I certainly did." I looked around towards the clock because I was not even sure what time it was. "You've certainly been a very busy man this morning."

"I want my Goddess to know that I am a worthy slave and I am here to please her."

I gave a slight shake of my head. There was a lot of last night I still had to process. I liked it all, but was not quite used to it yet. I was a black woman with a white man who called himself my slave. I smiled at the thought of some of the uptight millionaires I worked with and decided that this concept would throw them for a loop. Then again, some of them may secretly like it! I smiled at the thought and focused back on Xavier.

"I'm a little confused, Xavier. I think the only thing I had in the refrigerator was a few bottles of water and a box of baking soda. Where did you get all of the stuff that's wafting those good smells out of my kitchen?"

He walked over and knelt down in front of me. Then he bent down and kissed my toes. Taking my hand, he looked up into my eyes. "I had the groceries delivered, Goddess. I found a store near here on my phone and they were pretty quick about it. I also had them bring some fresh flowers. While I was waiting, I noticed that we had gotten the place in some disarray with our, um…activities last night, so I started cleaning. I was holding off on the vacuuming until you woke up. I did not want to disturb you."

As he finished talking, Xavier let go of my hand and leaned back on his knees. "Goddess, may I taste you quickly before you sit down for breakfast. I have been longing to do so since I woke up."

My head was still spinning a bit. I looked at Xavier. With his puppy dog expression, he looked like he wanted approval from his owner. *Actually,* I thought, *that analogy is exactly what is going on here.* I composed my face somewhere between stern and serenity and said, "Yes, you may. But only for a couple of minutes, that food smells too good to have it burn."

With that bit of permission, Xavier smiled and kneeled up straight. He opened the front of my robe and delicately kissed my pussy. I felt the kisses circle around as he administered his affection on both thighs. All of a sudden, I felt his tongue slowly make its way up my slit, and then slowly back to the center of my ass where he began to lick and suck there for a few minutes. I looked down and saw the top of Xavier's head slightly moving up and down between the draping of my robe. He sped up his tongue action and skillfully used his fingers, inserting them in and out. Simultaneously a surge of my essence filled my pussy as I reached down and pressed Xavier's face harder into me. Like a horse responding to the reins, he took this as a sign to go faster. He reached behind me, grabbed both butt cheeks, and drew me even closer, burying his head between my thighs. He added some suction to the licking and before I realized what was happening, I was exploding my wet juices onto his face and into his mouth. Xavier took his time drinking it in and licking up anything that started to trickle between my legs.

I released him and he straightened up on his knees, again with a big smile. His face glistened from the sticky, clear cum and suddenly the entire room smelled like sex. I felt a little wobbly in the legs and sat down. I looked at Xavier with his satisfied grin and simply said, "Slave, you just ate and now it's your Goddess's turn to eat. I'm famished."

Xavier leaped up off the floor. I could see that his massive dick was at full attention in his boxer shorts. *That's okay,* I thought, *he can stay that way for a time.* Out loud I said, "Xavier, from this point on, you belong to me, mind body and soul, and you know that from now on you only cum when I tell you too, right?"

"Yes, my Goddess, I am yours to command." With that, he scurried into the kitchen.

I heard a chorus of cutlery, glasses, and plates erupt from that direction, and soon Xavier emerged carrying one of my huge trays loaded down with a mountain of food. As he set it on the coffee table in front of me, I saw omelets, bacon, pancakes, French toast, sausage, fruit, fresh-squeezed orange juice and coffee. There was enough here to feed a family for a week. Xavier said, "I made all of this because I didn't know what you like."

He pulled the table closer to me so that everything was within easy reach. He then sat down on the sofa next to me and picked up my feet. He started to firmly massage them as I started eating. I looked at him over a cup of coffee and said, "Aren't you going to eat?"

"Yes, Goddess, when you are finished. I want to make sure that you are fully satisfied."

I almost choked on the coffee. Satisfied? I came so much last night that I still felt lightheaded. Throw in that breakfast appetizer Xavier conducted between my legs ten minutes ago, and I was about as satisfied as I had ever been.

All during my breakfast, Xavier never stopped administering to my feet. He occasionally broke up the massage by leaning down and kissing my toes or sucking on them one at a time. I felt occasional shockwaves erupt near my pussy. I was not even close to another orgasm, but it was as if he was fanning the fires down below with his constant massaging. I knew that if he kept sucking my toes, we were going to be quickly heading back to the bedroom for round two.

"Mmmmmm, Xavier this food is really good, where did you learn to cook like this?

"Thank you, my Goddess. Growing up, my Pop always cooked and my Mom wanted to make sure we could all survive on our own. I actually find it relaxing. There are times on the oilrig when I tell the cook to take a break, just so I can play around in the kitchen and prepare a meal. None of my mates out there ever seem to mind when I get creative on their behalf."

"I am full. That was absolutely wonderful." Xavier beamed at the compliment. "Now, after that and all of last night's shenanigans, I need to take a shower."

Xavier gave me his puppy dog look again. "May I help?" he asked.

"Just how are you going to do that?" I asked.

In reply, he stood up and extended his hand. I reached for it and allowed him to help me up off the sofa. He then led me into the bathroom. Letting go of me, he went over to the shower and started the water. He next rummaged through the cabinets and retrieved a couple of clean towels. He carefully placed the towels on the sink and once more took my hand and guided me into the shower.

I loved the delicacy and attention Xavier bestowed on me as he prepared the shower. I started to adjust the temperature. My body seemed to crave a really hot shower so I could feel completely refreshed. As I was getting the heat just right, I felt something press up against my back. It was Xavier entering the shower behind me. I turned and looked at his naked body inches from me. Glancing down, I noticed that his penis was only semi-erect, yet it still looked huge. For a moment I was distracted as I marveled at how he had completely filled me with that thing and how good it had felt.

Xavier brought me back to the present by asking what soap I liked to use. I chuckled because I had all kinds of bottles and tubes and bars on the shelves that dotted the inside of the shower. I was a girl who loved the feeling and aroma of being clean. What I used on any given day depended on my mood. Today, I picked up my favorite Alba passion fruit shower gel and handed it to him.

He immediately got on his knees. The water was pelting both of us, but he didn't mind it hitting his face. First, he gently turned me so I was facing away from him. Then, he slowly and methodically started to wash me. Even on his knees, he could easily reach my shoulders and this is where he began. He worked the gel up into a rich lather so that there were bubbles everywhere. I could feel his strong hands rub into my shoulders and down my back. He spent a long time doing this, taking his time. I idly wondered what a total body massage would feel like from Xavier. Just by washing my back, he was doing magic things to the knots in my muscles.

When he completed this area, he began to knead and wash my ass with complete concentration. I smiled when I started to feel him alternate the washing with some soft butterfly kisses to my bottom. I sucked in my breath as I felt first one, and then two, wet fingers enter me. This boy was certainly intent on cleaning me inside and out! I began to feel a wetness building up from this activity, which had nothing to do with the shower. Just as I thought I would give in to what was building up in me, Xavier stopped and began to thoroughly soap down my legs.

I took a deep breath and regained my composure. I put my hand up against the shower wall in front of me as I willed myself to calm down. Behind and below, I felt Xavier washing my ankles. Then there was a gentle touch on my hip as he silently directed me to turn around.

When I did, a quick glance, I noticed that he was once again fully hard. I carefully leaned down and wrapped my fingers around his thick cock and slowly began to squeeze tighter and tighter, he stared up at me wide-eyed, with the shower cascading down onto his face. I exerted a little more pressure and a mixture of pain and pleasure worked itself over Xavier's features. Finally, I released him and said, "Slave, you are doing a wonderful job cleaning me."

"Thank you, Goddess," he murmured as he bent over and kissed my water-covered toes. He made this movement seem effortless despite his size and the confining area of the shower. He then straightened up on his knees again and began washing my front, once again starting at the top. When he got to my breasts, he seemed to take an abundantly long time washing and rubbing them. Xavier made sure the nipples and underside of my breasts were particularly clean, and I felt my nipples getting hard. .

"Slave," I purred, "I didn't realize my breasts were so dirty!"

"I am sorry, Goddess. I could not help myself." Saying this, Xavier soaped up, washed my tummy, and then carefully proceeded to my vaginal area. Once again, I marveled at how he was determined to clean every niche on my body. The way he moved his fingers in and out made me moan with pleasure and made my knees weak from having another orgasm. I thought I was about to explode yet again when he stopped and moved on to my legs. I knew that Xavier was trying to get me to the edge so that I would want him. However, after last night, and despite the desire inside me, I decided I was not going to take on Xavier's cock again quite yet. Especially not after he had come without my permission.

Deciding it was time to take back control of the situation, I ordered Xavier to stand up. Towering over me, I told him that it was time for me to wash him. When he started to protest, I gave him a firm, "Shut up! Part of wanting to take care of me is to listen to me." I was sort of acting here, because this was still a little foreign to me. Still, I was pleased with the results as Xavier relaxed and stood quietly next to me. Well, almost relaxed…his cock stood straight out like some missile-awaiting launch.

Just as Xavier did with me, I started on his shoulders. However, with every motion I leaned in, mindfully pressing my breasts up against his hard muscular chest. I enjoyed washing him since he had such a beautiful body, like a chiseled statue. I looked up into his eyes as I tweaked his nipples. Looking for more of a reaction, I pinched them harder, one in each hand. His nipples began to turn red from the pressure. A shadow of pain flitted across Xavier's face as I began to twist them. Before it got too bad for him, I stopped. I then soaped and rubbed them to turn the pain into pleasure. He slowly smiled at me as he enjoyed the sensation.

Working my way south, I went over his firm stomach and then my hands settled on his genitals. I worked the gel up into hundreds of bubbles and rubbed them all around his cock and balls. I firmly grasped his dick with both hands and started to sensually pull on him. With constant delicate strokes, I applied my skill to see how close to the edge I could push him. A low moan escaped from his lips. I went a little faster and I could see that he was starting to sweat, even in the shower. I took one hand off his rod and started to slowly massage his testicles with my long nails digging into him. Xavier started to rise up on his toes with the added stimulation. I picked up my pace and dug my nails in deeper. All of sudden, I could feel his balls tightening up. At this signal, I immediately stopped, put a firm grip on his dick, and stood on my toes to get closer to his ear. "Remember," I whispered, "you cannot cum until I say so." I then slapped the tip of his penis and the surprising action made him jump but his cock got even harder. He let out a yelp and exclaimed, "Goddess, why are you doing this?" as he fought for control.

"Because I want to!" I explained.

I felt his cock take on a life of its own as it began to twitch and spasm in my hand. However he did it, he successfully kept himself from spewing his creamy liquid all over me. After a couple of deep inhales, he quietly said, "Thank you, Goddess. I am OK now."

With that, I spun him around, smacked his ass, and said, "Shower's over. If we stay in here much longer, we're going to turn into a couple of wrinkled up prunes." He turned the shower off, reached out to pick up a towel from the sink, and began to dry me off with the water still dripping from his body.

He kissed me on the shoulder as he reached past to take the towel from my hand. "I want to serve you," he said. "I do not want you to lift a finger or break a nail. Please let me take care of you."

I relented and let him dry me off slowly. I had never met anyone who wanted to be this devoted to me. Like the previous night, I decided that I might as well just keep going and see how long this ride was going to last.

As he was toweling off my legs, Xavier looked up and asked, "What would you like to do today?"

I said, "I haven't given it a lot of thought. I know I planned to head down to the mall. I have to buy a new dress for my friend's birthday party."

Xavier gave me his big smile. "That sounds like fun. May I come with you?"

I gave him a long look. A man who wanted to go shopping! What a concept. I nodded and said, "I think that's a good idea. We need to get out of here for a while."

Xavier quickly took my robe off the hook and helped me put it on. Together, we went to the bedroom. He had me sit on the bed and tell him what outfit I wanted to wear. Under my direction, he pulled out everything from underwear to shoes. I got dressed and Xavier requested the honor of putting my shoes on. When I agreed, he once again threw himself to his knees and picked up my feet. He gave both feet a quick massage, covered the toes in kisses, and secured my shoes.

He went back into the living room to where he had his clothes from the previous evening neatly folded. As he dressed, he had his cell phone in one hand and requested an Uber car to be waiting for us when we left the condo. I decided that he looked good both naked and dressed!

Together, we left the building and found the Uber car waiting. Xavier helped me into the seat and instructed the driver where to go. On the ride over to the mall, we quietly talked and laughed in the back of the cab just like any other couple. Anybody watching us would never have known what an intense and intimate time we'd shared over the past eighteen hours.

Once we arrived at the mall, we immediately headed to my favorite dress store. I said to Xavier, "I hope you are not in a hurry. I'm really not sure what I am after. I may be trying on more than a few dresses."

"No fears, Goddess," he said. "I'm not due back on the oil rig for another three weeks." He gave me a wink and a grin.

Knowing that I was not going to have someone telling me to hurry up, I took my time perusing the dresses. A sales lady stayed stuck to my hip as we chose different outfits and I went into the changing room to put them on. Xavier quietly sat and watched from one of the easy chairs next to the changing rooms. They usually held impatient men who were fuming while their wife or girlfriend was trying things on. Xavier, however, patiently watched as I went in and out, seeing how I looked in my choices.

Finally, I had it narrowed down to five dresses. They all looked beautiful on me and accented my best features. As I was heading back into the dressing room, I told Xavier, "I'm only getting one dress, but I can't decide which one. I have five I'm going to model for you, and I want your honest opinion of which one looks best. Can you pick which one you like best?"

"You know I will do anything for you. I promise I will give my honest opinion of which dress looks best on you."

With that, I went back in and put on the first dress. As I came out, I beamed at the look of admiration in Xavier's eyes. He gave some appropriate comments and said he would hold his opinion until he had seen me in all of them. As I went back into the changing room, I heard Xavier tell the sales lady to bring each outfit back after I had changed out of it. He wanted them hung on the rack next to him so he could keep all of the dresses straight in his mind.

The fashion show continued through all five dresses. I couldn't really tell from Xavier's reactions which one he liked best. As I stood there in my bra and panties in the changing room, I handed the final dress back to the sales clerk to put on the rack with the others. As I began putting my clothes back on, I realized I was very interested in Xavier's opinion. The man dressed well, had good taste, and could even cook. I might think he was gay if he wasn't such a stud!

As I emerged from the dressing room, I looked over to the chair where Xavier was sitting. The problem was, there was no Xavier…and the dresses were no longer on the rack. I quickly scanned the store and saw Xavier with the sales lady at one of the registers. I hurried over and was stunned to see Xavier hand over his credit card to the lady with instructions to wrap all five dresses!

I grabbed his arm and said, "Xavier, sweetie. I cannot let you do this. It is way too much."

He moved closer to my ear and whispered, "No, my Goddess, I want to do this. It is my pleasure. Please, I want you to understand that I *really* want to take care of you." He straightened up and said in a normal tone of voice, "Besides, you asked me for my honest opinion. I thought you looked smashing in all of them! How could I decide?"

Dumbfounded, I just watched as the woman behind the counter carefully bagged all of the dresses. When they were ready to go, I reached for them, but Xavier quickly intercepted them. "No, Goddess," he admonished me. "You might break a nail. No manual labor for you when I am around." He took my hand and we left the store.

Strolling towards the exit, Xavier spied Saks Fifth Ave with shoes near the entrance. Smoothly changing direction, he guided me through its doors. I paused once I was inside. This was a store where I would love to shop. It was full of top-of-the-line brands, like Gucci, Chanel, Jimmy Choo, Prada, and others. I was making a decent living at that time, but was still working my way up in the world of financial services. I was nowhere near having the "designer label" money I thought I needed to buy these shoes.

Xavier saw my reluctance and said, "Come on. We can have a little fun checking out the shoes. It doesn't hurt just trying some on. I could tell that you loved those sandals that were waiting for you in the car last night." I nodded, "I guess you're right. I have to say, I don't think my feet have ever been so happy as when they wore those Gucci's into the restaurant. The heels were high but they felt amazingly comfortable."

I started walking around the store pointing out styles and colors that appealed to me. A pair of black leather, peek toe, platform Gucci pumps. Then a sexy pair of light gold, glittery, textured leather Jimmy Choo sandals. And a pair of black, open toe, t-strap Christian Louboutin stilettos with red bottoms. A salesman, who was every bit as attentive as the woman in the dress store, hung on my every word. He made a note of those, and all the other pairs I liked, and asked my size. Then he led Xavier and me over to a love sofa and asked us to be seated while he went in the back. The other sales person offered us bottles of water while we waited. In a few minutes, the other guy returned with a half dozen boxes. As he got down on one knee to help me try them on, Xavier tapped him on the shoulder.

"That is fine, sir. I appreciate the help, but I will help the lady try these on." Xavier was smiling pleasantly and the salesman nodded his head in agreement. He was looking disappointed, as if he was looking forward to putting the shoes on my feet.

"Give me a call if you need anything else brought out or if you have any questions." The man gave a brief bow and went over to a section of the store where he could see if we needed him, but not be intrusive.

Xavier got down on his knees and helped me take my shoes off. Taking his time, he carefully placed each pair on my feet. His caresses on my feet and calf were having a physical effect on me. I felt my panties getting wet as my handsome Aussie pampered my feet. It struck me again how big and strong he was, but very delicate with his hands at the same time. I could also see that all the foot play was affecting him, and that his large cock was growing harder in his trousers. I playfully touched his cock with the tips of my toes, acknowledging his hardness.

Xavier encouraged me to walk around to model the shoes and see how each pair felt. I did just that and spent a lot of time admiring each selection in the mirror. They all looked like beautiful works of art framing my feet. Xavier asked me which ones I liked.

Sitting down to take off the last pair and to let Xavier put my shoes back on, I said, "I like all of them. But to be honest, the Christian Louboutin were not very comfortable, and I was not totally thrilled about the color of those boots. The other four pairs are amazing, though." Sensing that we were finishing up, the salesman hurried over and asked me what shoes I was going to select. Sensing my hesitation, Xavier said, "Choose your favorite pair out of the four. You deserve them!"

With that prompt, I pointed to the Jimmy Choos. I couldn't believe it. I'd received two gorgeous pairs of shoes in two days. I was not used to being spoiled like this, but I could certainly get used to it!

As we got up, Xavier mumbled something to the salesman. He then took my hand, picked up the dresses, and started to walk out of the store.

"I saw a little café a couple stores down," he said to me. "This nice young man is going to wrap your shoes. We can go get a smoothie or something. One thing shopping does do is make me thirsty."

We made our way over to the café and took one of the tables that sat outside in the walkway of the mall. Xavier draped the dresses over one of the chairs. As we sat down, a waitress hurried over to take our order. We both decided on iced tea. As we were waiting for our drinks, I said, "You cannot keep doing this for me. Don't get me wrong, I love it, but I do not even want to guess how much you spent today."

"Goddess, I will do anything you want or say. I will take care of you to your heart's desire. I only ask that you do not worry about anything I spend. My folks raised me right and I never spend what I cannot afford. Deal?"

I smiled at his earnestness, "Deal!"

Our iced teas came and we chatted about the different sites in Washington that Xavier still wanted to see. When we were halfway done with our drinks, Xavier looked at his watch and said, "I'll be right back. I just want to run in and fetch the shoes. Won't be more than a moment." He got out of his chair and strode powerfully back to the department store.

I watched him walk away, admiring his ass. My attention wandered to some of the other patrons of the mall. There was everything from families, to packs of teens, to some obviously wealthy shoppers. I sensed Xavier coming back toward me and I swung around. To my amazement, he was carrying two big shopping bags holding four shoeboxes, not just one. I tried to say something, but Xavier put the boxes on the table and put up a hand to stop me as he kissed me on the lips. "No, we just agreed not to say anything. Just know that seeing you happy makes my heart swell, Goddess."

I closed my mouth, stood up, and kissed Xavier on the cheek. "Why don't we get out of here and maybe I can thank you in private."

Xavier's eyes lit up as he started to gather up the multitude of bags containing the dresses and shoes. He resembled a packhorse with all of that stuff, I thought. I knew it was pointless to offer any help, so I led the way out of the mall with Xavier trailing behind. Once outside, we got an Uber and were soon back at the condo.

As we entered, Xavier insisted that I do nothing. I went to sit on the sofa as Xavier scurried around and carefully put all the packages in the bedroom. He came back out and took my shoes off. He spent five minutes massaging the soles of my feet, and when he applied pressure to certain areas it sent shockwaves throughout my whole body. He got up and busied himself in the kitchen for a few minutes, and came back out with a fruit tray loaded with cherries, green grapes and apples that he placed in front of me. He told me to relax and enjoy while he put all of the purchases properly away.

After the rustling died down in the bedroom, Xavier came back out and sat down at the other end of the sofa. He picked up my feet, put them in his lap and began his expert massaging. I leaned back with my eyes closed for a few minutes and enjoyed the relaxing and sensual manner in which he manipulated my feet. Opening my eyes, I murmured, "I know I said I wouldn't question your spending, but I am curious about where you get all of your money."

"Working on the oil rigs is high risk work, Goddess. They pay all of us very well. In addition, I receive extra because I am an engineer and am now the manager. That's why I can order the cooks out of the kitchen whenever I fancy," he said smiling. "Now, Goddess, I have a question for you. Do you mind that I have a foot fetish?"

I responded, "I have heard of foot fetishes, but I am not all that up on the definition. How do you describe your foot fetish?"

"I love feet, pure and simple. I love how they feel, how they smell, and everything else about them. I receive sexual pleasure by giving massages like this," indicating what he was doing to my feet. "There is nothing sexier to me than a woman with a fresh pedicure."

"So, you admire my feet like other men admire my breasts?" I asked.

"I guess that's one way of putting it," Xavier said. "But don't get me wrong, I also find your breasts quite exquisite!"

I smiled, "Good to know. I do try to keep my feet looking beautiful. I continue getting pedicures even in the winter."

"How did you know to give me a foot job, Goddess?"

"I just saw how you reacted when I stepped on your cock and took it from there. It was instinctive when I saw the amount of pleasure you were feeling."

Xavier said, "You are what is known as naturally dominating."

I started. "Why do you say that?"

"Because you dominate without really trying. You naturally knew what to do. That is why you are so special and why I was so attracted to you. You are unique in so many ways. Not only are you beautiful and sexy, but also you have that aura of domination about you. How did you know I was into CBT?"

"I didn't. "Dominique laughed and asked, "What does CBT stand for?"

"Cock and ball torture. That's why I went wild when you stepped on my dick. How did you know to do that?"

"It was an accident. I just continued when I saw how much you loved it. Something seemed to take over and I knew exactly what to do."

"Like I said, Goddess, you are a natural!"

I saw Xavier's eyes light up as he said this. I leaned over to him and in a silken whisper said, "It's time."

Without waiting for a word from Xavier, I hopped up and went into the bathroom. I wanted something to put around his cock. I found a heavy-duty rubber band that I sometimes used for my hair. I concealed it in my hand and went back out to the living room. I straddled Xavier, hiding the rubber band behind my back.

He asked, "What do you have in your hand?"

Xavier's question jolted me into Goddess mode. I grabbed his hair, snapped his head back, and shouted, "You do not question your Goddess. You only talk when I ask you to speak and you only cum when I give you permission."

Xavier meekly nodded, at least as well as he could do when someone was yanking on his hair. Inside, I was amazed. Here was this strong and tough Aussie in the palm of my hand. He was totally submissive to me. This turned me on so much that my pussy was starting to get soaked.

I opened up Xavier's pants. Seeing his big, thick dick made me wonder how I got all of it inside me last night. I quickly took the rubber band and wrapped it around my fingers to reduce the size. I slid it down his shaft. When the rubber band closed around his cock and balls, Xavier's eyes went wide with the pain. Knowing I had to take his mind off the discomfort, I slowly started to stroke him with a firm grip. I leaned over and whispered into his ear, "Whose cock is this? Whom does it belong to?"

Xavier didn't answer right away, so I squeezed harder and moved my hand faster. I asked the question again. This time Xavier blurted out, "It is yours, Dominique. My heart, my body, my soul belong to you Goddess."

The way that he said "Goddess" with his Australian accent triggered something inside me. I felt the animal in me coming alive. I stood up and stripped off my clothes. I positioned myself over Xavier's cock and slowly slid down on it. The rubber band was acting as a cock ring and making his already big cock feel even bigger than it had the previous night. I put this thought out of my mind as I slowly flexed my hips up and down. I grabbed Xavier's head and pulled his lips onto the nipple of my right breast. As he sucked on it, I felt myself sliding further down his cock. It began to go deeper and deeper inside of me.

I could see the pleasure in his eyes and this made me rock my hips even faster. I finally felt his dick all the way inside of me. Xavier grabbed my hips and stopped me from moving. I pulled his head back by his hair again and commanded, "You only stop when I tell you to stop!"

Xavier exclaimed, "Goddess, I am going to cum!"

I leaned over and bit his lip. "Your cock will learn how to listen to me. I told you already, you only cum when I say so." I could see the anguish in his face. He was concentrating very hard so as not to explode. My tight pussy was sliding up and down his huge penis and its width stretched out my pussy to the max. I could never remember feeling so full. I didn't know when I had ever felt this way.

My huge breasts were bouncing in front of Xavier's face. He closed his eyes in an effort to control himself. The Goddess in me ordered, "Open those eyes and look at me." As he did so, I stood up, spun around, and lowered myself back on his cock, reverse cowgirl style. He now had a view of my ass bouncing up and down in front of him.

This position allowed his cock to go in a little deeper and I felt myself starting to cum as I moved my hips faster. When the juice from my orgasm hit Xavier's cock, he grabbed my hips and moved me up and down on his dick even faster. Inarticulate grunts came out of his mouth, like a savage beast. Suddenly, I could feel his cock thicken and I knew he was about to cum. He sensed it too and to prevent himself from cumming without permission, he actually picked me up and pulled his cock out. Now, when I am about to cum I love it when the man keeps pounding me hard to keep the orgasmic waves flowing. So I hate it when he stops to prevent himself from cumming, which ruins my orgasmic pace, as I have to wait for him to catch up. I was so angry at his lack of cum control that I slapped his cock to teach him a lesson. This slap was the point of no return for Xavier and he shot stream after stream of cum all over me.

Things began to calm down and my legs stop shaking. I looked down at Xavier who was slouched back in the couch looking a little glassy-eyed. His cock was still erect, hard, and pulsing. I gave him a sharp slap in the face. I said, "First, you are going to clean this mess off me. Then we are going to have a little training session so this doesn't happen again."

****

Dominique's retelling of this story was getting her hot and bothered again. She had to drink a cold glass of water to calm herself down. Meanwhile, Veronica, who was hanging on every word Dominique spoke, had been unconsciously squeezing her legs together as she imagined the scene Dominique described.

"What's wrong?" asked Dominique.

"I don't believe it. My panties are soaked just from the thought of it." Veronica glanced around. "At least with my pantyhose on, I don't think anyone will notice. But it is uncomfortable." She laughed. "In a good way."

Dominique smiled, "So you find this entertaining?"

"I am loving every word. I can't wait to find out what happened after Xavier shot all over you. Was it a lot?"

"It looked like someone had spilled vanilla ice cream all over me," said Dominique. Speaking of something sweet, I think I'll try one of their white-chocolate covered strawberries." Dominique got up and headed over to the dessert table.

Veronica slowly shook her head in disbelief as the "Goddess", as Veronica was beginning to think of her, got up and walked away. Veronica noticed that men in the area followed Dominique with their eyes, even if he was sitting with another woman. Veronica wondered if she could command that type of attention from men in the future.

Chapter 4

Veronica was still wondering if she had a Goddess inside of her when Dominique returned to the table. As she was sitting down, Veronica asked her, "I have to know. What did you do when Xavier came all over you? Did you whip him or something?"

Dominique laughed, "Settle down, girl. I didn't have any whips…at least not yet. Remember, this was my first real exposure to having a man wanting me to treat him like this. As you've heard, I certainly wasn't shy about taking on that role, but I was making a lot of it up as I went along. I'll tell you how the rest of that weekend went. Then we may want to call it a night. We both have work tomorrow."

"Good point. But please tell me what happened when he exploded on you."

Dominique thought for a moment and then continued her tale of that wild weekend with Xavier.

****

I was genuinely mad at him for his failure. After he had sheepishly run into the bathroom to get a washcloth and towel to clean me off, I told him to get on his knees and crawl to the corner of the room. There, he was to kneel and think about why he was being punished like a bad little boy. I warned him that if he moved or uttered a word, he would feel my fury, once again

I spent the next few hours going about my life and totally ignoring him. He stayed right where he was like a good, little soldier. I spent my time taking another shower, watching television, and re-inspecting the dresses and shoes Xavier had bought for me. I gave him high marks for the way he neatly put all of the purchases away in my walk-in closet. My anger was beginning to calm down. I took off my clothes, put on my red robe from the closet, and stretched out on the bed. Soon I fell into a short, but deep sleep. My last twenty-four hours had been incredibly intense and all the activity with Xavier, plus the shopping, had worn me out. I needed to recharge my batteries.

I woke up feeling refreshed, and I smiled thinking about Xavier still sitting in my living room. I got out of bed and crept over to the door. I peered through, and much to my delight, Xavier was still sitting where I'd left him. He had remained naked and had his hands folded in his lap. He looked like a little boy at detention in the principal's office. Well, except for him being naked and the huge dick dangling between his legs.

Xavier sat up a little straighter when he heard me coming toward him. I ran my hand along his face. "Do you know what it means to be a good boy now?"

"Yes, Goddess," he said. "I can only cum when you tell me to. I am so sorry. I just could not help…"

I cut him off with a gesture. "Stop, as long as you understand. Now, this is what we are going to do. You are going to head back to your hotel."

Xavier's face fell when he heard this.

"Get that look off of your face. I want you to go back, shave and shower, and get some clean clothes. I think these," I indicated the pile by the sofa, "are rather wrinkled and dirty by now." You will come back here at seven and pick me up. There is a little Italian restaurant I love in Georgetown, and we are going to go there and have a nice dinner. I forgive you for your earlier insolence, so we can have a fun, relaxing time there.

"Oh, Goddess, I am so happy. I would enjoy that immensely. And I will show you what a good boy I can be.

"We'll see. After dinner, we'll return here. Maybe I need to do a little more training with you." I reached down and fondled Xavier's cock and balls. To my surprise, the rubber band was still there. My touch immediately started an erection. "We are going to train your dick to be worthy of your Goddess and for it to do exactly what I want!"

"Yes, Goddess. I think that will help a great deal. I will do my best to meet your expectations." Xavier was almost gushing. He smiled and stood up and reached for his clothes.

I touched his arm. "And, Xavier, you can take the rubber band off."

He returned to my place right on time. I knew he was devoted to pleasing me, but he had trouble controlling his cock. I was going to do my best to help him with that. After dinner and a nightcap at a bar, we returned to my condo. Dinner had been light, fun, and friendly. Now that we were back at home, I laid down some ground rules. I said, "You will not talk unless I tell you to. I demand complete obedience. And you damn well know that nothing better come out of your cock without my permission. Do we understand each other?"

Xavier shyly nodded. I could immediately see that his cock grew hard in his pants when I said this. "Now, take your clothes off and stand there."

I sat back in my sofa and watched Xavier quickly undress. He folded his clothes and placed them on a nearby chair. He came over and stood right in front of me with his cock almost touching my nose. I quickly gave his dick a sharp smack and said, "Back up! When I want that in my face, I'll tell you."

Xavier retreated a couple of steps, and stood there with his arms by his sides. I took a leisurely time looking over his body. He was a handsome dude. He had a nice face, strong chest and shoulders, and very muscular legs. Once again, I marveled that I was able to take that monstrous cock all the way into me more than once. I got wet thinking how it sounded when his balls were smacking my ass as I rode him after our shopping expedition. I knew I would feel him again, but first I had to teach him some self-control. I channeled the anger I was starting to feel as I remembered his cumming without permission and ruining my orgasm. I jumped up, wrapped my hands around his balls, and gave them a squeeze. I looked in Xavier's eyes as I felt his knees buckle a little.

"Now, Xavier, I am going to make you feel good. You are going to get very excited, but there better not be a repeat of this afternoon's accident." I let go of my grip. "Now, stand up on the coffee table."

I knew that my table was solid and could hold his weight. He tentatively stepped up and stood there. I walked over and slowly circled the table. I stopped behind him, admiring his ass. I took my hand and applied a stinging slap. The sound echoed around the room and Xavier lifted slightly off his toes. I admired the red mark on his butt, and how his ass muscles clenched upon impact. I also thought his cock got just a bit more erect with the whack.

Coming back to the front, I grabbed Xavier's dick and squeezed. "Did you like me hitting your ass? You may answer me when I ask you a direct question."

"Yes, Goddess, I did," Xavier whispered.

"Why?"

"I love anything my Goddess wants to do with me."

"Hmmmm," I hummed. I silently contemplated what I had in my hand. With my left hand, I exerted pressure on his cock and bent it down. As a slight groan escaped Xavier's lips, I brought my other hand up to smack his balls. Looking at his face, I enjoyed seeing the look of pain and pleasure pass over him. I applied a little more stress to his genitals and stopped when I saw Xavier's face turn beet red. I let go and said, "You will stand there. I will be back."

I retreated to my bedroom and took my time undressing. There was no reason to be in a hurry. Xavier wasn't going anywhere! I looked at my naked form in the mirror trying to decide whether to go out there nude or with something on. I decided on the white robe from the bathroom and slipped my arms into it. Then I picked up some items I had collected from around the condo after Xavier had left for the afternoon. I brought them out and placed them on the sofa. For what I had in mind next, I realized that Xavier was at the perfect height standing on the table. There had to be one small adjustment, though.

"Step down, Xavier."

He did so. I took two of the bandannas I brought out with me. I took the dark blue one and blindfolded him. I instructed him to put his hands behind his back and I securely bound his wrists. He gasped as I tightened them together. For as long as I could remember, I could tie things up better than anyone I knew. Where many people would get nervous with such treatment, Xavier still stood strong and his cock began to stick straight out again.

I said, "Get back on the table." I took his elbow and guided him up. Then I continued, "It is time for a little instruction, Xavier. You disappointed your Goddess earlier today."

"I am so sorry, Goddess, I…ahhhhh!" Xavier's comment ended in a yelp as I smacked his ass with the wooden shower brush I had also brought out.

"That was not a question! Who told you to talk?"

"Nobody, Goddess. Sorry."

"I am beginning to get sick of your 'sorry.' Now, I am going to have some fun with you. It will be painful, but I think you will enjoy it. But you cannot cum until I say so.

With that, I went to work on Xavier's genitals. First, I softly caressed them. I took a little bottle of baby oil off the sofa and put a light sheen over Xavier's cock. I gently cupped his balls and slowly stroked his dick back and forth. I could feel it growing in my hand. I realized this was the first cock I'd ever had that I couldn't close my hand around when it was in all its glory. I smiled at the drop of pre-cum that appeared at the head. I continued stroking it, in an almost loving manner, as I took my other hand, reached up, and twisted Xavier's right nipple. The sudden explosion of pain made Xavier gasp and his cock inadvertently twitched out of my hand.

I yanked down on his arm forcing Xavier to crouch. "You better not cum. I was nice last time you disobeyed me."

"But, Goddess, when you do that…" Xavier flew off the table into the sofa as I wound up and smacked him in the side of the face.

I put my face up to his and screamed, "No talking, damn it!"

Xavier whimpered. I yanked him up to a standing position on the floor. I took a black bandanna and went to work on his cock and balls. With a few deft movements, Xavier's junk looked like a calf that was lassoed and tied up at the rodeo. I gave an extra tug to my final binding and Xavier cringed.

"Stand there, slave," I yelled and sat back on the sofa to catch my breath. I admired my handiwork. Xavier looked incredibly uncomfortable, but there was a slight smile at the corners of his mouth. I'd bound up his penis and testicles so his dick could still stick straight out. It was so hard it looked like it could punch a hole in a cement wall.

"Come stand in front of me." Xavier maneuvered himself over to where he heard my voice. I put a little more oil on his dick and went back to stroking. It seemed that with each rub, Xavier got more excited. The drop of pre-cum that was on his dick turned into a steady dribble of essence. His face was getting redder again, but not from pain.

"That's a good boy," I cooed. "Your Goddess will tell you when to cum. You must work on your control. You do not want to cum in your Goddess before she is ready, do you?"

Xavier mumbled out, "No, Goddess. I want to please you. I always..." The rest turned into inaudible gasps.

Deciding to up the ante, I stood up and shed my robe in one motion. Continuing my jerking of Xavier's cock, then I pushed him down on the sofa and pulled the head of his dick into my pussy as I gave Xavier a deep, passionate kiss. The poor man's dick felt like it was about to go off. I was just about to stop when he yelled out and shot his cum over my stomach, up to my tits, and over my shoulder. There had been no warning and I looked at the goo that coated my hand. I saw red. Didn't this guy get it?

I was furious. I punched and slapped Xavier several times, then put both hands on his chest and pushed him as hard as I could. With his hands tied behind his back and blindfolded, he lost his balance and tumbled off of the sofa. As I stood there catching my breath, I could have sworn his cock was already getting hard again. I shook my head, picked up my robe, and went back into the bathroom to clean up.

After a half hour passed, I came back into the living room attired in my robe and slippers. I leaned over and removed the blindfold and other restraints. Straightening up, I tossed a blanket at him, pointed to the couch and said, "Sleep there. I do not want to hear one damn thing from you until you bring me breakfast in bed at 9:30. Goodnight!" I turned on my heel, walked into the bedroom, and slammed the door.

Sunday morning started with a very contrite Xavier bringing me another breakfast feast, this time in bed. I mentally noted that it was good he was still naked since I hadn't told him to get dressed. After I finished eating, I ordered him to clean up the kitchen and prepare me a bath. I let him sit on the toilet and watch me as I luxuriated in a bubble bath for an hour. I blatantly ignored him the entire time.

Starting to feel a bit waterlogged, I said, "Please hand me my towel. As I'm drying off, I want you to go and sit quietly in the living room."

Xavier did as he was told. I dried off and wrapped myself in a towel. I strolled out into the living room and confronted Xavier. "Tell me, slave, have you learned your lesson?"

"I have, Goddess."

"Instead of shooting your nasty cum all over the place, wouldn't you have enjoyed putting my cock," I reached out and grasped it, "into your Goddess?"

"Yes, Goddess, that is what I want."

"Lay down on the floor."

Xavier carefully spread himself out on the floor. I straddled his chest with my legs. I took off the towel and flung it away. Looking past my breasts, I stared down into Xavier's eyes and said, "You certainly had your pleasure last night, but I did not because of your selfishness. You are going to make up for that now."

With that, I plopped my pussy down onto his face. "Now! Eat me, slave until I cum. You will do it until I tell you to stop."

Xavier went to work with his mouth and tongue like a man possessed. He quickly got me worked up into a froth. I felt my juices flowing down and around his face. I had not been kidding. He got off twice yesterday and I had to keep myself from cumming so that I could punish him appropriately. I started rocking my hips on Xavier's mouth. The first roiling tide hit me as I yelped and flooded my slave's head. I heard some gurgling under me and I yelled for him to keep doing it.

I opened my eyes and saw Xavier's cock sitting straight up like a stone monument. I reached forward and grasped it. I started jerking on him and said, "You will not cum."

I felt another orgasm building in me and I cried out as I released. It felt like we were playing in a pool, since everything was so wet! I saw Xavier's ass bouncing off the floor due to my work on his dick. I stopped jerking it, held it tight, and said, "No! But keep licking my pussy." I ground down harder. Turning to take a quick look, I saw his face getting red. I eased up a bit and leaned forward to let him breathe a little better. In this position, I took his cock into my mouth. There was a strangled cry below my pussy when I did this. I let his dick slide out of my mouth as I hit my third orgasm. They seemed to feed my body into just wanting more of them.

Looking at Xavier's cock, I knew what I wanted. I thought, "Let's see if he's got the concept of control down yet. Because if not, I might have to kill him!"

I sprang off Xavier's face, nimbly spun around and came down on his cock with my pussy. I gritted my teeth as I plunged down on it. I knew I was as wet as I could get, so I hoped this would work. I cried out as I once again felt like I was being split into two. I threw caution aside as I rode Xavier as fast and as hard as I could. Xavier could not believe how fast my ass was going up and down. Finally, with a guttural cry, I had my fourth and best orgasm in the last twenty minutes. My cum oozed down Xavier's cock and over his balls. I kind of fell to the side and looked back at him. His eyes were glazed and he had a smile of triumph on his face because he'd controlled himself.

I patted his throbbing cock, "Good boy. We are going to tie that up for a while, but your Goddess will make sure you cum later. I am proud of you."

****

Dominique looked over at Veronica. Her hand was down in her lap and she was sweating. It even looked like her glasses were fogging up a bit. "Easy, girl," Dominique said. "We're in public."

Veronica shuddered as she got control of herself and self-consciously put her hand up on the table. She took off her glasses, fanned herself with a napkin, and drank down the last of her wine. "That was incredible. Did he maintain control of himself for the rest of the day?"

"He did. There was one other time he almost lost it but I think what saved him is that he had cum so many times that he had nothing left. But all of those other times, he only came when I told him he could. We fucked and sucked and everything else for the rest of the day. I finally told him to go back to his hotel at around dinnertime. I was worn out and I had a big presentation to give at work the next day. I took a long, hot bath and collapsed into bed. I was worried I'd be walking around like a cowboy the next day since I fucked that huge cock so many times, but I was fine. At least nobody could tell my pussy was so sore."

"I'm going to have to go home and break out one of my toys," said Veronica. "If I had a guy in my life I'd be riding him tonight until he couldn't stand it anymore. I feel like my pussy is on fire."

"That's good," said Dominique. "Embrace your sexuality. That's the very first step to making the changes you want. You are a woman and a guy is not going to take what he wants from you anymore. You decide who to you give yourself to and when."

"I have to wrap my head around all of this. I'm going to have visions of you and Xavier in my head for the rest of the night."

"No hurry on anything," said Dominique. "I want you to know you can ask any questions you want at any time. This is all a process. I do like how you reacted to it all." She stood up. "We should get out of here. Tomorrow is a workday. Give me a call when you get a chance and we can get together for more of your, uh, education."

Veronica stood up and hugged the other woman. "Thank you, Dominique. I'm so happy you came into my life."

They left the restaurant together, hugged once more and headed off in their different directions.

Chapter 5

*A*fter having a restful night sleep, Dominique arrived at the office a few minutes early. She liked to start the week off on a good note on Monday, catch up on emails and client calls, etc., but mainly review her calendar for her weekly reminder of priorities. While knowing full well that with some of her more demanding clients her priorities could change with the first phone call. Dominique proceeded to immerse herself into the work she loved.

The day flew by and suddenly; Dominique realized it was time for lunch. Whenever possible, she tried to get out of the office to eat. Even if it was a quick meal, the mental break did wonders for her. She was contemplating if she wanted to grab a bite with any of her colleagues or eat alone when her cell phone buzzed. Looking down at the display, she smiled when she saw it was Veronica.

"Hello, Ms. Lady," she said as she answered the cell. "Did you spend much time thinking about the stuff we talked about last night?"

"Oh my God, Dominique," Veronica gushed. "When I got home last night, I played with myself for an hour before I was calm enough to sleep. I wanted to call my ex-boyfriend; I would have given anything to have a real man. I was so horny."

Dominique chuckled. "Now, Veronica, I told you about what happened for educational purposes. I didn't mean to get you all hot and bothered."

"You told the stories so vividly. It was like I was rewinding them on a TV screen in my head last night. The more I got myself off, the more I felt like this is whom I am. I think this desire to be in charge is really deep inside of me, but I want to do what you can do…one of these days!"

"Don't forget, sweetie, it took me some time to even get to the point I told you about last night. I have learned so much more in the seven years or so since then."

"I'm patient, Dominique. I'm also an excellent student. Learning about this is much more interesting than all of the college courses I took combined!"

"And just like college, you need to master all the prerequisite courses before you move on to the advanced knowledge. You have to crawl before you walk. Life is the best lesson."

"I know. I really want to hear more about you and Xavier. I hope I'm not being a pain, but when can we meet up again?" Veronica asked.

"You're not a pain," answered Dominique. "I am quite enjoying this. You know, I do a little bit of volunteer work here and there to educate women on how to empower themselves in the workplace, but I never really thought about helping them to completely empower themselves like this. For me, I don't differentiate who I am at work and in life. If I can help you discover the woman you are; then I'll believe I've done a really good thing."

"Dominique, I believe you certainly know what you are doing and I feel like you've opened up some vault that I had closed deep inside of me. I'm not sure what to do with all of these new ideas and urges yet, but as I said, I'm patient. In time, I think you can help me."

"I'll certainly do my best," said Dominique. "Do you have anything planned this evening?"

"No, do you want to get together again?" Veronica asked eagerly.

"Sure. Tell you what. Let's make it a little more casual. I usually head to the gym after work on Tuesdays. Want to come over to my place around seven thirty? We can have a drink and I'll fill you in on what happened with Xavier."

"I can do that," exclaimed Veronica. "Let me bring some food over and we can eat. Do you like Chinese? There's a place near me that's excellent."

"Sounds like a plan," said Dominique. She gave the younger girl her address and told her what Chinese food she liked.

Hanging up, Dominique smiled. She really liked this girl and enjoyed the role of mentor and teacher. Dominique loved the thought of women uplifting women. Within society, women very often tore each other down. So many times other women had not liked the fact that Dominique's presence commanded attention, and had resented her for that. It was nice to see that a woman actually could appreciate her attributes. Dominique had learned to love and to accept herself for who she was. She knew that other women who were confident and comfortable with themselves would appreciate a friend like her. She was a little hazy on where these meetings with Veronica were going, but she would just trust her instincts. They had rarely failed her in the past.

With that, Dominique stood up and stretched. She took a long look outside her window and decided to get something to eat on her own. It would give her a chance to think about what she would talk to Veronica about tonight. She smiled when she realized that replaying the next adventure with Xavier in her mind would make for a pleasant lunch. She gathered up her jacket and left her office to head out to the same restaurant where she'd first met him.

Promptly at 7:30 pm, Dominique's doorbell rang. She was drying off after taking a shower. She'd had a good workout at the gym and felt good. She wished she had a dollar for every man, or woman for that matter, who gawked at her while she was working out. Her gym clothes did nothing to hide her voluptuous figure…not that she tried. All in all, she felt great and grabbed a ruby red robe to wrap around herself to answer the door. It was a short wrap that stretched just a couple of inches past her ass and barely contained her breasts.

Dominique dressed in this on purpose. She realized something she needed to do was to show Veronica how comfortable she was in her own skin, and that it was acceptable to exude sexuality. She wanted the young woman to start realizing that about herself. Besides, after a strenuous session at the gym, Dominique was fine with wearing very little or nothing around the house. It felt very comfortable tonight.

She opened the door and said, "Hello, Veronica. Welcome and come in."

The young girl stood there in black jeans and a yellow windbreaker over a blue sweatshirt. She was holding a large, brown bag that had white, cardboard containers poking out the top. Her mouth dropped open a little and her eyes widened behind her glasses before she caught herself and said, "Hi, Dominique. I guess you just got home from the gym?"

"No, I've been home for a half hour but I just came out of the shower. Come in. Let's go to the kitchen and we can get some plates."

Veronica followed the red clad Goddess through the townhouse. It was big and tastefully decorated. Veronica saw a good-sized living room and a formal dining room that was right off the kitchen. A hallway joined the living room and Veronica assumed it led to the bedrooms. She put her bag down on the counter and said, "This is beautiful, Dominique. I could tell the entire complex was very nice when I walked up. Downtown Arlington is such a nice area. How long have you been here?"

Dominique thought for a minute. "It's been about five years now. I had a nice condo before this, but I upgraded, as business got better. This is bigger than I had before. It has two bedrooms, an office, and two and a half bathrooms. I like it."

The two women opened up the takeaway boxes, containing chicken fried rice and triple delight. Dominique got out a couple of plates and they helped themselves. She suggested they go sit in the living room to eat. She also grabbed two glasses and a bottle of Estancia, her favorite wine, to wash the food down.

As they ate, Veronica and Dominique exchanged stories on how work was going and the latest gossip in their respective offices. Veronica found herself slowly getting used to Dominique being so exposed and her eyes took in the other woman's features. "She is beautiful," thought Veronica, "I'll never have tits and an ass like that." She looked down at her own dowdy clothes and gave a silent sigh.

The food was good and the women were getting more comfortable with each other. When dinner was done, they put the dishes in the sink, closed up the food containers, and put them in the refrigerator. As they headed back to the living room, Veronica asked, "May I use your bathroom? Then maybe I can hear more about you and Xavier."

"Absolutely," said Dominique. "Go down the hall there and it's the second door on your right. She settled herself in her seat on the couch as

Veronica headed off for the hallway.

Dominique had just started to take a sip from her wine glass when she heard the girl explain, "Oh wow!"

Hurrying into the hallway to see what was wrong, Dominique saw that Veronica had accidently wandered into her dungeon. Technically, it was the second bedroom, but Dominique referred to it as the Dark Room. One of the reasons Dominique wanted a bigger place a number of years back was so she could have a full-fledged playroom. "Oh well," she said to herself, "I guess I'm going to do a little more educating tonight than I planned."

The room became softly lit when Veronica turned on the lights. Turning to Dominique, she stammered, "I think I went into the wrong room."

Dominique gave her a big smile. "Is that right? I was going to save this for some other time and give you the tour. But since you're here, I can give you a quick look around."

The room was painted completely black and there were dark blinds that prevented any light from entering, thus giving the appearance of a dark dungeon. It was about twenty feet long and ten feet wide. When Dominique had first seen this particular townhouse, she knew immediately that the dimensions of the room suited what she wanted to do with it. She had painstakingly furnished and decorated it over time. It had a good amount of equipment, shelves, and cabinets in it, but it did not feel cramped or crowded. Dominique always smiled when she thought of her dungeon as "cozy." Not a word usually associated with such rooms, or what went on in the room, but it fitted her fun chamber.

Veronica was wandering around with a dazed look on her face touching different pieces. She was breathing heavily and Dominique thought it was because she was either overwhelmed or slightly excited by the room…or both. Veronica touched an intricately designed metal ring mounted to the wall. It was seven feet tall and made of steel. The ring had metal crosspieces throughout it that were solidly welded into the round frame. She asked, "What is this?"

"It's called the Pendant," said Dominique. "The idea is that with all of those metal pieces, you can tie or strap someone to it in all kinds of ways. They can be standing, sitting, or whatever you decide. It's also big enough to attach two to three people to it. Besides the practical aspect, I thought it had a cool design."

"So you have tied men to this?"

"Oh, yeah. They all loved it. When you have someone so restrained that they cannot move no matter what you are doing to them, the effect is mesmerizing and intense."

There was a stand-alone wall in the room with an adjustable hole at waist height that slid up and down. It also had different sized holes arranged in a circle, and handcuffs dangling from the top. Veronica asked, "What in the world is this and how do you use it?"

"Well this is my spin on the glory hole. I secure my victim behind here." And with that she grabbed Veronica to demonstrate, cuffing both of her hands to the wall. It was so fast and smooth Veronica didn't even have time to object before she realized she was pinned and helpless. She suddenly got an inkling of the fear Dominique's slaves must have felt when they were in her place. "Now," Dominique continued, "once he's is in place I adjust the hole to fit his height and then the dial here with the different holes is adjustable to fit any size dick. Once he's inside the hole I blindfold him and my fun begins." Dominique smiled as she gave Veronica a slight tap on her ass and then uncuffed her.

Veronica silently nodded and went over to another piece of furniture. It stood about four feet tall and looked a little like a table. The padded top was only about six inches wide, though, and four smaller padded sections were halfway down the legs and attached to the front and rear of the table. "This looks interesting."

"It is. You lie on the top on your tummy and rest your arms on one set of those pads and your knees on the other. Get up and try it."

Veronica gave her a long look for a moment and did as instructed. The padding was comfortable and she saw in a mirror on the wall that her ass was up in the air. She let out a little yelp as Dominique playfully swatted it. "Imagine that you are a guy up there like that. If you are naked, I have full access to everything. Some men really like having their ass spanked and even fucked. There are some toys over in that cabinet for things like that. Sometimes I get up there when I want it hard and fast from behind. I've had some good times on that thing."

"So it is not just for torture?" asked Veronica.

"No, not torture, just pain and pleasure, however, there is a very thin line between the two. You have to start thinking about it differently," said Dominique. "One person's pain is a lot of pleasure for someone else. I'd like to think that I exhibit my domination in a sensual way. That's the thing you have to remember about everything I've told you so far. Xavier wanted me to do all the things we did, and I got pleasure from doing it. At that point in my life, I never would have thought about slapping or stepping on a man or his dick, but when I saw how much he loved it when it accidentally happened, it became part of our activities. Besides," she continued with a smile, "I have been thoroughly fucked on that thing and believe me, it was not torture." At least not for me. It may have been for the man who was deep inside my pussy and ordered not to cum until I told him to."

Veronica giggled and hopped off the bench. She went over to a section of the room that had two hanging devices. Both were made out of leather straps and were on pulley systems. The first one was two simple straps with loops in the end. Veronica reached up and put her hands through each loop. "Let me guess. You strap a man's wrists in this thing and then pull it up till he is barely touching the floor or dangling, right?"

"You catch on fast. Unlike the ring over there, this allows you to walk around the guy and torment him from all sides. Personally, I love having men blindfolded when I use this. I think it makes them feel extra vulnerable and heightens their pleasure. There is something pleasing about seeing a suspended man with his cock sticking straight out. You certainly feel a sense of power when you are playing with a guy in that state. I remember teasing a guy so mercilessly here that when I lightly touched his ass with this," Dominique picked up a purple and black riding crop off of a shelf, "that he shot his cum all over the floor. It was something to see. I still had to punish him for cumming without permission, but I got turned on watching him. Good thing he had a blindfold on so he couldn't see that I liked that."

Veronica reached over and played around with the intricate combination of straps on the next device. Some were rather wide and she was imagining how they all worked together. She shook her head and said, "I give up. How does this operate?"

"It's actually pretty simple. That is a sex swing. Let me show you." Dominique maneuvered herself so that she was reclining in an almost horizontal position on the leather. The thicker straps went under her back and ass and there were two straps to rest her feet. As she climbed into the swing, her robe opened and Veronica had full view of Dominique's beautiful breasts with their big nipples and her shaved pussy. It dawned on Veronica that she really was with a Goddess. She had seen many naked friends over the years, but nobody was as awesome as her new mentor. After a moment she realized that Dominique was talking. "…Not so much a torture device as for my pleasure. I love hanging here and having a man inside of me. It's almost what I imagine having sex in outer space is like. You are just floating free without the trappings of this physical world and being fucked so hard and deep it becomes a spiritual sensation."

Dominique motioned for Veronica to help her out of the swing. Veronica dutifully came over and stood in front of Dominique. She couldn't help but stare at Dominique's body just like she had seen countless men staring in the bars they had been in. But she was able to behold this Goddess in all her naked power, and she was overcome by the raw animal magnetism Dominique's body inspired in her.

Dominique noticed Veronica staring and decided to push the girl's limits a little bit. "Can you wrap your arms around my back and give me a lift?" Dominique had a way of making a question sound like a command and Veronica instantly obeyed. As she rubbed her hands across Dominique's smooth caramel skin for the first time, she felt herself wanting to do it slowly to absorb the pleasure and sensuality of this scene, not only with her sense of touch, but deep in her mind as well. As Veronica lifted Dominique up, their breasts came into contact and Veronica felt a jolt of electricity dance through her body. She was amazed at how the mass of Dominique's natural G-cups made her D-cups look small and insignificant in comparison. She wasn't ashamed at the sudden thought she had of caressing Dominique's perfectly round globes and even putting her mouth on those succulent nipples! Veronica was barely able to control herself as she lifted Dominique out of the swing. She had been given a mere taste of this Goddess's power and she had almost been overwhelmed with desire. She could only imagine what one of her s felt, as he was bound and helpless at the mercy of such an elemental force as Dominique.

Back on her feet, Dominique rewrapped the robe around her and secured the tie as if nothing had happened. "As I said on the phone this morning, you need to learn the basics first. This is the advanced class." She gave one of her big smiles. "I want you to get comfortable with who you are and allow your imagination to go wild." She swept her arm around the room. "This stuff is fun to play with, but your biggest sex organ is up here," Dominique tapped her head. "When you can access the goddess in you, your power over a man is only restricted by your brain."

"I can see it's going to be difficult getting to sleep again tonight. My mind is going to go wild imagining how to use this stuff. I have seen some BDSM porn, but this makes it so real." Veronica fingered the swing. "I'm getting wet thinking about being on this thing with a man doing what I tell him."

"Before you get those jeans soaked, why don't I show you the right door for the bathroom? Then we can go get comfortable again and chat."

"Sure. Sounds good." Veronica reluctantly let go of the swing and followed Dominique out. She went into a beautifully decorated bathroom. Taking down her jeans, Veronica felt how wet her pussy had become. Her fingers went to her clit and she quickly massaged it. It didn't take long for her orgasm to hit. She muffled her groans with the sleeve of her sweatshirt and then calmed down enough to relieve herself. She washed her hands and splashed water in her face. Taking a deep breath she looked at her breasts which had, up until a few minutes ago, seemed huge. But after seeing Dominique's G-cups, she suddenly realized just what huge really meant. Her D-cups were still pretty good, she thought, and were certainly big enough to put her in the Goddess category. Dominique was a great friend to have as she exuded self-confidence and empowerment and, unlike most women, did not put others down but instead raised them to her level. Veronica felt calm enough to walk back out and face Dominique for her next lesson on her path to being a Goddess. Veronica realized she had been in the bathroom for a few minutes and hoped Dominique didn't guess that she had needed to cum after touching Dominique's body. She could certainly understand why Xavier had cum in two seconds after touching Dominique as well.

She made her way out to the living room where Dominique smiled up at her from the couch, "Feel better?" she asked with a grin.

"Um…yes." Quickly sitting down she said, "Your bathroom is very nice too. I really like your place." It was Veronica's turn to smile. "Right down to the dungeon."

"I could tell you enjoyed that. I guess seeing it helps make all of this seem a little more real. Here you go. I refilled your glass. Sit back and I will tell you about my next adventure with Xavier."

****

Xavier and I spent endless hours together and the sex got more interesting and fun. Little by little, I could sense that he was becoming more and more submissive to me. Each time we went to my home, our play became more intense. I fucked his dick raw. It was to the point that he would want to rub my feet, suck on my toes, or lick my pussy for hours, rather than have sex with me. I saw him rubbing his cock with aloe lotion to try and soothe himself.

That didn't bother me. I wanted to push him to his limits. For the rest of that first week together, I experimented with different ways of teasing and torturing him. I found intricate ways to bind up his cock and balls. I got very good at bringing him to the brink of cumming, and then stopping at the very last second. There was one time when he shot all over me without permission and I had to severely reprimand him again. I think, though, that it was the last time he ever did that. He was so willing to please me.

Friday night of that week was my friend Jessica's birthday party in Alexandria. She always threw the best parties. She would hold summer barbeques, Christmas parties, and events throughout the year. Jessica was beautiful and smart. She spent a lot of her time working with a nonprofit agency that helped developing countries in Africa. She also worked part-time at a cozy, local bar called Bilbo Baggins in Alexandria, which is where we first met each other.

At the party, I decided to step up my game with Xavier. I put on one of my new dresses and a pair of shoes from our weekend shopping spree. The dress was a subtle-blue silky number I loved. It softly covered my breasts but the cut was such that when I moved, the material threatened to uncover the girls. It never did, but it had that sense of danger I like in clothes. The heels I wore were so comfortable that I felt like I was barefoot in the sand. They did wonders for my legs since the dress was short enough to reveal my toned calves and thighs.

I was so proud to show off my Australian man to everyone. Xavier was as dapper as ever in a light-brown suede sport coat and chocolate brown slacks. He wore stylish loafers and looked like he was ready for a fashion shoot with GQ magazine. Xavier always made me think of the high-powered lawyers we have in this town with the way he dressed. You would never look at him and think, oilrig!

Throughout the party, Xavier sat next to me and attended to my every need. He spent the first part of the evening fetching me drinks and appetizers. He did not want me to move a muscle. When he went over to the hors d'oeuvres table, Jessica congratulated me on my find. "Dominique, he's gorgeous. And I love his accent. I wish I could find a man who would be that attentive to me."

"Sorry, I couldn't find you one for your birthday. Hang in there and keep trying. He kind of fell into my lap."

Jessica arched her eyebrows. "I am sure he is doing more than that in your lap. Have fun, honey. I'll be back with you later."

As Xavier came back toward me, I thought it was time to put my plan in motion. As he handed me a plate of food and bent down to kiss me on the cheek, I told him to go get me another drink. As he went to the bar, I headed to the bathroom. Inside, I lifted my dress and took off the black thong I was wearing. I carefully folded it and put it in my purse. It felt fun and naughty to re-enter the party going commando. I was looking forward to Xavier's reaction to what I was going to do next.

When I came out, I noticed the single women flocking around Xavier. He quickly noticed me and cleared a path as he came over and escorted me back to my seat. I loved how I was always the focus of his full attention. I never noticed him eyeing another woman, even though I pointed one out to him on the dance floor who had a big ass and huge tits. He took a quick glance at her and said, "She can never hold a candle to you. Your beauty surpasses these mere mortal women because you are a Goddess!"

I leaned over and whispered in his ear, "I have something for you." I slyly pulled my thong out of my purse and placed the black lace in his hand. He quickly smiled at what I handed him and then he gave me a quizzical look. I fiercely whispered to him, "Now, go and put it on".

His eyes went as wide as his smile. I kissed him on the lips softly, but passionately and said, "Xavier, don't keep your Goddess waiting." I got up and walked around mingling with my friends. I watched Xavier out of the corner of my eye. He sat there motionless for a second as he worked up the courage to accept the emasculation his Goddess was demanding of him. He knew this was the next step in his evolution and headed in the direction of the bathroom.

I was dancing with a friend when I felt Xavier behind me. He grabbed my waist and I turned so that I could dance with him. I reached out to run my fingers along the top of his pants. I slipped my fingertips into his waistband and felt around. I smiled with delight when I felt the lace of my thong around his waist. This turned me on more than I thought it would. I enjoyed the power I had over him. Now I knew that Xavier would please me in whatever fashion I desired.

We continued to dance as if we were the only ones in the room. I grabbed him by his ass and pulled him close. I felt his dick getting hard against me. I knew I wanted him right then and there. I reached up, guided his head closer to me, and kissed him. I rolled my tongue in his mouth and sucked his tongue very gently. I quickly stopped and told him to meet me in the bathroom.

As I walked quickly towards the hall, I could feel moisture dribbling down my leg. I didn't even have underwear on anymore to stem the flow. I glanced over my shoulder and saw Xavier trailing after me surreptitiously. I slipped into the bathroom and closed the door, keeping my hand on the handle. After a few seconds, I heard a light tap. I opened the door wide enough for Xavier to fit his body through and then quickly closed it.

As soon as he was inside, Xavier grabbed me and started to lift up my skirt. I moved his hands off me and began to unbutton his pants instead. "Let me see how sexy you look," I said.

He smiled and replied, "I love dressing sexy for you, Goddess".

I told him, "Yes, I know you do because you are my sexy bitch!"

"Yes, Goddess. I'm your sexy bitch to do whatever you ask of me."

He looked great in my thong. His gigantic cock was testing the strength of the fabric as it stuck straight out from his body. I decided to tease him, so I turned around and lifted up my skirt. When Xavier saw that I had no underwear on, he lunged at me. I told him, "You can put that thing in me for a count of ten strokes. And I want to hear you count each thrust out loud."

Fortunately, I was so turned on that my pussy was soaked. I gasped as I felt the usual penetration of his steely cock. I could feel him fill me completely up. I tried to control my breathing as he started to count. When he got to five, he slowed down the count and his thrusts. I almost squealed each time he slid up into me; it felt so good. I could feel myself begin to cum and I knew that if I did not pull him out, I was not going to stop. Just as he was pulling back ready for the last thrust I quickly reached around and pulled his cock out. Xavier begged me to put it back in for number ten. It took great willpower on my part to say, "No, Xavier, you are going to have to wait. I have a special surprise for you when we get home." With that, I pulled down my dress and smoothed everything into place. My man was still standing there with my cum dripping off his cock. I gave him a quick kiss and left the bathroom. I took my seat and after a few minutes saw a slightly dazed-looking Xavier opening the door to the bathroom and walking back towards me. No one seemed to notice that we'd been in there together.

He walked over to where I was sitting holding his jacket in front of him. I figured it was to hide his hard-on. He took my hand to pull me up and said into my ear, "Let's go."

I did stand up, but gave him a big smile and said, "I'm not ready to go yet. Let's stay a little longer. I'm having fun." I could have sworn I heard him give out a little moan as I walked away.

Xavier followed closely behind me. It was as if he could not keep his hands off me. He would stand behind me and grab my waist or bend down to kiss me on my neck. I pulled his hands down to his sides and sternly told him, "I will let you know when I am ready to go. Do not rush me again!" Then I smiled and gave him a kiss on the cheek. My problem was that when I did this to him, it was difficult to hide just how much I wanted him as well.

After my warning, Xavier took care of my every need. He fetched water for my friend and me when I asked. He continued to bring over appetizers and he made sure that my wine glass was never empty.

Throughout the rest of the evening, I could tell that he was still excited from our bathroom encounter. I loved the fact that there was this sexual aura surrounding the two of us, but nobody else at the party had any clue to what was happening.

My friend Jessica put on more music and she and I started dancing. Xavier stood there watching the two of us grinding close together. I finally reached out and pulled him onto the dance floor. I turned around and rubbed my big ass up against his hard cock. As we danced, I shook my ass faster and faster. Xavier grabbed my waist and pulled me closer to him where I could feel his full erection against my pussy. I played along and continued to tease him by dancing very sexy and twisting down slowly. I could feel his hands firmly on my hips. I then pulled away and, smiling, looked him right in his eyes. He took this as a cue to grab me close and start to kiss me. I was thoroughly enjoying myself and Xavier liked my teasing him. We both were getting tipsy and having fun.

The entire time we stayed at the party after our bathroom encounter, I made sure that Xavier's dick stayed hard. I gave him credit for dancing in that condition. I loved feeling his lust for me drip off him like someone sweating in the sauna. He was so obedient, and I thoroughly enjoyed showing him off to my friends. I knew a few of them were trying to figure out how I got this gorgeous man to be my virtual slave.

He constantly begged me to leave as he tried to control himself and keep his hands from touching my body. It got to the point where I was so irritated by him constantly asking to leave, I told him that every time he asked, I was adding twenty more minutes to our stay there. He lowered his eyes in that sad, puppy-dog look until I finally said that we were leaving. With that, he perked up like a beagle about to take off after a fox.

****

Veronica kept licking her lips so much that Dominique stopped her story and asked, "How are you doing, sweetie?"

"I'm sorry. Each story you tell me about you and Xavier is hotter than the last one. I thought I was going to lose it when you were telling me about him fucking you in the bathroom. I love your nerve and how he did whatever you wanted."

"I just took advantage of the situation and used my imagination. As you may know, usually the man initiates so much of the sex. The great thing is that when you have a man who can be your submissive, you do not take away any of his urges. However, you turn everything else upside down. Xavier having to wait for me to decide when we were going to fuck only got him hotter and hotter. It certainly made everything we did more intense and satisfying to me."

Dominique got up and refilled their wine. She smiled. She had to admit that reminiscing about that night was getting her wet too. She would probably scratch her itch later on, as she was sure Veronica would be doing.

Chapter 6

$\mathcal{V}$eronica made her way back to her chair from the bathroom. "That party was intense," she said.

"It was," responded Dominique, "but that was only the warm-up. You ready to hear what happened for the rest of the night?"

Veronica took a drink of wine as if to fortify herself and said, "I'm ready."

Dominique composed her thoughts and started to talk about the remainder of that epic night.

****

Xavier held my hand tightly as we exited Jessica's house. The night was cold but clear. Xavier had called a cab and it was now waiting for us outside. I couldn't wait to get him in the car, but walked unhurriedly with my escort. His affection for me gave me a warm feeling all over. I was still horny as hell, but I was going to bide my time.

Xavier opened the rear door of the taxi and carefully settled me in the seat. He ran around to the other side and climbed in next to me. He told the driver my address and the car pulled away from the curb. I took off my coat and placed it over Xavier's lap. I unbuttoned his pants and sensually massaged his hard dick through the material of my black thong that he was still wearing. They were very wet from his pre-cum. For a few minutes, I didn't say anything but continued to tightly squeeze his cock and fondle his balls. His breath started to come in ragged gasps as I kept working on him.

All of the sudden I clamped down on his balls. I felt his cock get even harder while at the same time, tears started trickling out of his eyes. I leaned over and quietly said into his ear, "You will never rush me again like that when we are out. Who are you to decide when and where we go? Always remember that I am the Goddess. You look to me for direction and orders." I squeezed even harder. "Got it?"

Xavier squeaked out, "Yes!"

I said, "Yes, what?"

"Yes, Goddess!"

I released his balls. Xavier let out an audible gasp of relief. He stayed hard, but sweat broke out on his forehead as his body recovered from my assault. He sat there quietly like a little boy whose parents had just scolded him. He kept his hands by his side and looked straight ahead for most of the trip to my condo. As we got closer, I went back under my coat and found his cock. I peeled away my thong from around it and slowly stroked him back to full hardness. I loved pushing him to the edge. It really empowered me to have that control over him. I whispered into his ear, "You remember how you came the other day without permission?" He nodded.

"You know, I thought we took care of that last weekend. I'm warning you right now that you had better not do that tonight, or ever again." My grip tightened on his cock. "You will learn to listen to me, your cock will obey. I know you want to, but now I am telling you that I do not think you want to pay the price for ever disobeying me again."

I remembered how hot it was to have that huge penis inserted into me in the bathroom at the party. It took all my self-control to stop, because all I wanted to do was ride Xavier right then and there until I had orgasm after orgasm. I am sure my yelling would have tipped off my friend as to what was going on in her bathroom, though. Jessica certainly would have had a birthday to remember if we did that. I could feel myself getting wetter thinking about what I had in store for Xavier when we got home.

A couple of blocks away from the condo, I released Xavier's cock. He struggled as he tried to maneuver his piece of steel back into his pants. The driver pulled over to the curb. Xavier leaned forward over the seat and handed some cash to the driver. Hopping out of the taxi, Xavier ran around to the other side and opened my door. Since my eyes were level with his crotch as the door swung wide, I could see the huge bulge in his pants. I accepted his hand to help me out onto the sidewalk. I draped my coat over my shoulders and we headed to the door of my building.

As we went in, I had to exert more self-control. I wanted nothing more than to have him ravish me. I knew that's what he wanted to do too. Tonight, though, I had some other things in mind that I wanted to try. On one of my lunch hours that week I had ventured into a store selling sexual novelties, toys, and other merchandise of pleasure.

I remembered when I was younger and my parents would punish me with a whipping. They would send me out to get a thin branch off a tree, which my father would ominously refer to as a "switch". If the switch broke as I was being punished, then I had to go out and get an even bigger one. I thought it was time to use this same concept on Xavier! He certainly had the temperament and need for that type of treatment from me.

Venturing into the sex store was as exciting as shopping for dresses and shoes. I took my time exploring all its wares and selecting what I wanted to buy. I had done a little research on the Internet before going to the store, so I had a general idea of what I was looking to buy. I guess I was mildly surprised at seeing so many different toys and sexy clothes hanging off the racks in one place. It was fun going through there and taking some mental notes on what I wanted to try in the future. Just shopping in there was getting me excited. I could feel the wetness begin to grow between my legs. I tried to imagine the rush from actually using some of the stuff.

I was looking forward to Xavier seeing my purchases. I felt like a little girl on Christmas Eve with the anticipation of getting my hands on him. As we closed my condo door behind us, Xavier did what had become his custom that week. He lowered himself to his knees, bent down and began to kiss my feet and rub the back of my calves. He exclaimed, "Goddess, I'm ready to worship you right now!"

I ordered him to hurry up and take off my shoes. Then he was to get undressed and take everything off except for my thong that held his package snug. We went into the living room and Xavier did as he was told. He looked magnificent with the black lace around his waist that struggled to contain his cock and balls. I walked over to him and cupped his package with my hands. He felt hot to the touch. I gave him a slow and passionate kiss and said, "Get on your knees and wait for me. I will be out in a few minutes."

He settled himself on his knees next to the couch. I went into my bedroom and took out my new purchases. First, I wanted to put on the sexy outfit I bought. I slipped off my dress and held up the sheer, full-lace bodysuit for a moment before putting it on and looking at myself in the mirror. It hugged my entire body from my shoulders to the tip of my toes. The material covered my arms to the wrists and had a plunging neckline that dipped all the way down to my belly button. A piece of the fabric draped off the jumpsuit that I could attach to my ring finger. I slid on the Gucci shoes he brought me the first night we went out to dinner. It added a flowing look to the outfit and I was very pleased with the result. I could already imagine Xavier's reaction to it when I walked out into the living room.

I grabbed the bag I had carefully put together before we went out, and sauntered back out to Xavier. A smile lit up his face as he saw what I was wearing. I walked back and forth in front of him, exaggerating my hip movements like a model walking the runway. I gave him a close-up view of my pussy and ass as I spun around directly in front of his face. I looked down and saw his cock twitching in my panties.

He looked at me and said, "Wow, Goddess, you look amazing!"

I smiled and then slapped him across his face. "You only speak when I tell you to. I am getting very annoyed at how you so quickly forget our past lessons."

"I am sorry, Goddess…"

I slapped him again. I bent down, put my face an inch away from his, and roared, "There you go again. Did I just tell you to speak? I don't think so! You do that again and I am taking this beautiful body back to my room and going to bed. Do you want me to do that?"

Xavier started to speak, but caught himself. With a beaten look, he just shook his head.

"Much better," I purred. I went into the kitchen and poured myself a glass of wine. I took my time since I wanted Xavier to reflect on his mishaps. I realized he really was pissing me off by forgetting the rules I laid down. I obviously had a little more work to do to break him.

I went back into the living room. I pulled out all of the items in the bag and laid them out on the table. The first thing I did was to choose a blindfold and tied it around Xavier's head. He started panting and breathing heavily as I took away his sight. His cock perked up in the thong. I cupped his face with my hands and said, "There were times on the cab ride home where your dick got soft. It is worthless to me when it gets like that, you know. You give me no choice, but to punish you."

He started to plead that he did not know what to do. Before he could mutter another word, I smacked him in the face again. This time I left my handprint behind. "Damn you," I screamed. "You are talking again. Do not talk for the rest of the evening unless I direct a question to you. You will learn your place!"

Xavier just knelt there quivering a little. I slapped him again. "That was a question. You can answer that."

"Yes, Goddess."

"Good. I want to make sure you are finally clear on all of this."

Xavier just nodded. I knew he was a little uncomfortable when wearing a blindfold. I backed away from him a little and went back to the table. I picked up a black leather-riding crop that was eighteen inches long with a strip at the end. I started walking around Xavier lightly smacking my hand with the crop. He seemed interested at the sound. "Sooooo, you like the taste of my cum. Are you a cum slut?"

Xavier meekly nodded.

I brought the crop down hard on the couch next to Xavier. He jumped at the sharp crack. I yelled, "I asked you a direct question. Answer me!"

"Yes, Goddess. I like the taste of your cum."

"Do you like the taste of your own cum?"

"No, Goddess"

"Well, that is too bad. If you cum again without permission, you will be eating your own cum off of me or wherever it falls. Do I make myself clear?"

"Oh yes, my Goddess," he said in a shrill voice.

I slowly traced his profile with the crop. I started at the top of his head and let the leather play around his forehead and then over to his ears. I slowly touched the bridge of his nose and dragged it down until it touched his lips. I traced the outline of his lips with the edge of the crop. Suddenly, I brought it down quickly, but lightly on his shoulder. It was just enough to sting. An audible yelp came from his mouth and I saw he was trying to hide a smile. I could see his cock liked it too, as it strained my thong to the breaking point. I figured that thing was never going to fit me again, as it fought to keep in Xavier's dick.

I went back to the table and picked up something I had been dying to try on Xavier. It was called the Humbler. The Humbler is specifically designed to restrict the movement of a man to keep him on his knees. This one was finished in black lacquer over a wooden base. It is a fully adjustable testicle cuff device that clamps around the base of the scrotum. I needed to secure the thing behind Xavier's thighs at the base of his buttocks. When he was in it, he would have to keep his legs folded forward as any attempt to straighten them, even just slightly, would pull directly on his balls, causing considerable discomfort.

"Xavier, get on your hands and knees," I told him. When he did as ordered, I placed the device on the back of his thighs and pulled his balls back. I forcefully pushed them through the opening and heard him gasp. I felt his cock getting harder and harder. He was enjoying all of this. I grabbed his cock and began jerking him off. I steadily went faster and faster. "You should always be on your knees like this in my presence."

"Yes, Goddess," he grunted. I could see he was trying to deal with all of the painful and pleasurable sensations I was putting him through.

I then asked in a faux sweet voice, "Do you want to lick my pussy, slave?"

"Yes, yes, Goddess," he said.

"Do you deserve to lick my pussy,?

Breathing hard, Xavier said, "No, Goddess, I do not deserve that. But please let me taste you. I want to please you."

As I pulled on his cock harder, I could tell I was getting him to the edge of an orgasm. His face was turning red and he was breathing hard to try to calm himself down. I stopped what I was doing. His face was priceless as he went from sweet agony to puzzled frustration. Before he could react, I stripped off the body outfit I had on. I got down on all fours and backed myself up into his face. With my outer pussy lips touching his mouth, I asked innocently, "How does my pussy smell, slave?"

"It smells like the sweetest nectar," he said.

"Do you want to taste it?"

"Yes, Goddess."

I scooted away from him and laughed. "Just because you want something does not mean you'll get it."

Xavier looked crestfallen. His tongue hung out of his mouth as if he was searching for my pussy with it. His balls were looking a little blue in the Humbler, but his cock was sticking straight out in his current position. I stood, picked the crop back up, and walked behind Xavier. He looked so helpless there with his ass sticking up in the air. He certainly could not move fast with his balls secured like that.

He went very still as I slid the tip of the crop down the crack of his ass. I slowly pushed and prodded when I got around his hole. Then ever so gently, I ran it around his restricted testicles. I gave them a smart slap with the leather strip on the crop. He sucked in his breath as he tried to maneuver himself into a comfortable position. Not really thinking about it, I drew the crop back and slapped him sharply in the ass. Below me, Xavier let out a yelp.

"I think you are beginning to realize just how much you are in my power, slave. How do you like being totally submissive to your Goddess?" I slapped his ass again to punctuate the question.

Xavier groaned and said, "I love it, Goddess. It is what I want."

"Good boy." I hit his ass again with a ringing slap. I straddled his back and lowered myself on to it. "Feel that puddle forming on your back, Xavier? That's how excited you've got your Goddess. I could have had you take me in the bathroom at the party, but I decided you needed more self-control lessons. My pussy is for me to decide who is in it and when. That is never a decision for you to make. Always remember, you cum for my pleasure, not your own." I took each end of the crop in my hand and put it over Xavier's head. I placed it under his chin, exerted some upward pressure, and lifted his head. "You do understand that, correct slave?"

"Yes, Goddess," he spurted out.

I relaxed the crop and got off him. I stepped back in front and sat down with my legs spread open. I could see the wet spot I left on his back and the juices seeping out of my pussy. I said to Xavier, "Come forward. I have a little something for you."

My slave crept forward the best he could in the Humbler. He made his way between my legs and his nose directed him in a beeline for my pussy. Before I could say anything, he assaulted it with his mouth and tongue. I almost came immediately, but fought for control. I extended my arm with the crop and brought it down hard on his buttocks. I could see a welt quickly starting to form.

"Enough," I screamed. "Who told you to attack me? Do you just want me to leave you like that for the rest of the night?"

"No, Goddess. What do you want me to do?"

"I want you to come forward and gently lick my pussy. I want you to explore me with your tongue…slowly. If you get too frisky, I will hit you again and we are done for the night."

With that warning, Xavier came back to my pussy and did exactly as instructed. I could feel his hot tongue exploring the folds of my pussy. My juices emptied into his mouth, which he greedily slurped up. I shuddered as his tongue zeroed in on my clit. I relaxed back on my elbows as I enjoyed the sensations that shot through my body. I was tempted to grab his head and pull him harder into my pussy, but I refrained. I wanted to see if he would continue to do what I told him. He did, and kept up the same pace as his tongue worked on me. He was breathing hard and I knew he wanted more. Finally, I shuddered with an orgasm and pulled away. I did it so suddenly that Xavier fell on his face. He yelled a little as his sudden movement made the Humbler pull on his balls. He quickly adjusted himself back into a more comfortable position.

I made my way back to my feet. My legs were trembling from all of the excitement and the orgasm. I looked down at Xavier. His face was soaked from working on my pussy and he kept shifting his position to get more comfortable. He froze as he felt the crop in the crack of his ass again. "That was good slave," I murmured. "See, you can do exactly what your Goddess wants. That is how I always want you to be."

I withdrew the crop and backed away. As quietly as I could, I tiptoed away from Xavier and headed to my bedroom. When I got to the doorway, I sang out, "Come here now, Xavier. I am ready for my slave to come and have his Goddess's pussy. "

I stood quietly, leaning against the doorframe. Xavier was maneuvering his large body around trying to get to the sound of my voice. He started to scuttle on the floor like a beetle as he headed to the bedroom. I covered my mouth so I wouldn't giggle as I saw him run into some of the furniture with his head. But, like any animal on an instinct-driven mating ritual, Xavier plowed on. I had a warm sensation go through my body watching him, and I could feel the wet moisture of cum trickle down my leg. As he crawled around the room, he tried to reach up on the couch, but because of the Humbler, it pulled at his balls. He let out some agonizing grunts of pain, but I noticed his cock was still hard so it gave him some kind of pleasure. After observing him searching for me for several minutes, I was ready to be fucked. I slipped into my room and got on the bed.

Making myself comfortable, I yelled out to the other room so he could follow my voice.

"Xavier, my pussy is dripping wet. It is actually running down my leg. I guess you don't want my pussy anymore. I might as well just go to bed and fall asleep."

I saw him come through my doorway on his hands and knees. He made it to the bed and tried to climb up. The Humbler prevented him from being able to make the ascent. I said to him teasingly, "It's a shame to let this wet pussy go to waste."

He then reached his right arm up on the bed and touched my boobs. He slid his hand down my body until he reached my pussy. He began to finger me. His hands were big and his fingers filled me up. After a week of practice, he knew how to hit all the right spots. His fingers felt as good as his tongue or cock would have. The curve of his fingers hit my g-spot and I could no longer control myself. I yelled out and had a massive orgasm that gushed out onto his hands. I came long and hard and wanted to be fucked. I needed Xavier's enormous cock and I needed it now!

I quickly hopped off the bed and unlatched the humbler. Xavier breathed a sigh of relief when I took off the device. I stripped my thong off him and took off the blindfold. Xavier blinked at me in the light. I saw his eyes take in my body and finally settle on my pussy. One of his hands went down to unconsciously rub his freed balls. His cock was glistening from his pre-cum and it was hard enough to pound nails. However, the only thing I wanted it to pound was me. I leaned forward and kissed him, which Xavier took as a signal that it was permissible to touch me.

He grabbed my legs, put my ankles above his shoulders, and leaned into me, shoving his dick ball-deep inside of me. We both let out ecstatic cries as our worlds collided. My pussy instinctively clenched down in a defense mechanism at the monster cock invading me. He started to pump his hips faster and faster, in and out. I was so turned on that I rocked my hips back on him simultaneously.

I could tell he was on the verge of cumming because he slowed down. I screamed at him, "Don't you dare slow down! If you slow down your punishment will be far worse then what happened today. And don't cum!" Something came over him because he switched to another gear and began to pump harder and faster than before. In fact, of all the fucking we did that week, this was the most intense ride he'd ever given me. I think my voice was just one continuous moan as I exploded over and over as I came. The different orgasms seemed to stretch into one continuous earthquake in my body as I poured bodily liquids all over Xavier, myself, and the bed.

I did not want him to stop. I continued shouting out commands of "don't stop," "fuck me harder," and "fuck me faster." Xavier responded to all of my orders. I felt like my body was slipping into another dimension with all the sensations shooting through it. I was aware of the loud slapping of his balls against my ass with every thrust he made. Every push seemed to expand my pussy further than it had ever been before. I could see his face getting red from the exertion.

With a yell, I leveraged Xavier up and put him on his back in one fluid motion. We hardly broke rhythm. In this position, I could drive my cunt down on his dick. I felt like he was reaching up to my cervix with every down-stroke I made. His hands reached up for my tits. He squeezed them and I felt his fingers rub my nipples. This set off another electric shock deep inside me and I felt the floodgates open again. I gasped as my pussy convulsed around his cock and I had another mammoth orgasm. I reached down, grabbed Xavier's head, and pulled his mouth up to my breast. He clamped on to my left tit and his mouth stimulated me even more. With one last tremor, I screamed out and fell forward on Xavier. I lay there with his arms around me. My body shook and shuddered for minutes as I tried to calm down. His large cock was still inside and my pussy continued to spasm. I just lay there for a long time in post-sexual bliss. At that point in my life, I had never been as excited or as thoroughly fucked out as I was that night.

I finally picked myself up off Xavier. When my pussy came off his still solid dick, I swear it sounded like a cork popping out of a bottle of champagne. I looked down at my exhausted slave and gave him a long, deep kiss. After a few minutes, I slid off his body and sat on the side of the bed. I thought about getting up and heading to the bathroom, but my legs were wobbling so much I didn't think they would hold me.

I smiled at Xavier, "After all of that, you did not cum. Good boy."

"I knew I was pleasing my Goddess. There was no way I was going to ruin the moment by shooting into you. I was afraid of what you would do to me."

"As well you should," I said. "Maybe I'll let you cum tomorrow due to your good discipline."

After that, we cleaned up a bit and slipped back into bed exhausted. I spooned into him with my back to Xavier. He surrounded me with his big strong arms and we drifted off into a deep sleep.

****

Veronica's dark-brown hair hung in front of her face as she sat bent over on the chair, looking intently at Dominique. She was silent for a minute as she took in the entire tale. Shaking herself out of the zone she had put herself into, she reached for her glass and gulped down the rest of the wine. "Oh…my…God!" was all she got out.

Dominique took a deep breath to calm herself. It was exciting to relive that wonderful night with her new friend. She felt her pussy throb with the memory of Xavier's dick on its unrelenting assault of her insides. She sighed a little because, like Veronica, she could certainly use a cock inside of her after all this talking about it.

She gathered herself and said to Veronica, "Well, what do you think?"

"Honestly, I have to process all of this. I feel speechless and a little lightheaded. And I do not think it's the wine." She contemplated her empty glass. "When you tell me your stories, it's like I'm there. Sometimes watching, but at other times it's as if I am you. I can feel myself getting wet and I want to feel a stud of a slave fucking me!"

Dominique laughed. "It was an experience. It was that night when I knew what Xavier had told me earlier in the week was true. I was a natural domme. Yes, I did a little research on toys and how to use them but when I was in the moment, I never felt any hesitation. I just knew what to do."

Veronica sat up straight. She pulled back her hair and looked intently at Dominique. "How will I know if I am a natural?"

"You'll really get an idea when you have a guy you want as your slave. So far, though, you love what we've been discussing and are hot to trot to try it all at some point. Give it a little more time. You barely have your learner's permit with this lifestyle. You're not ready to drive by yourself yet."

A smile crossed Veronica's face. "Yeah, I know. But I do know I want to be in the driver's seat at some point. I'm looking forward to it." She stood up. "I guess I'd better head out. It's getting late and we have work again tomorrow. Thank you so much for your time and hospitality."

"Hey," said Dominique, getting up and hugging Veronica, "thanks for the Chinese food. I enjoyed taking a walk down memory lane just as much as you enjoyed hearing it. Let's face it. If we had a couple of guys here right now, they would be spent trying to please us. I don't know about you, girl, but I am horny as hell."

Veronica picked up her jacket. "No disagreement there."

Together they walked to the door. Dominique opened it. "You get home safe. Text me when you get there and we'll talk soon." As she closed the door after Veronica, Dominique smiled. That party sure had been one hell of a night.

Chapter 7

$\mathcal{T}$wo days later, Dominique was having a stressful day at work. It was midmorning and she had just spent the last hour meeting with one of her clients for the annual review of his portfolio. His investments were doing quite well. In fact, it made him so happy that he spent the last fifteen minutes of their meeting trying to entice Dominique to come visit him at his DC condo later that evening. It did not matter to him that his wife was at their horse country mansion in the Hunt Valley area outside of Baltimore. He thought of himself as the ultimate alpha male and he could not understand why Dominique was not throwing herself at him.

For her part, Dominique wondered why she did not throw this little shit out of the window. Then she looked down at the summary sheet, saw how much his account made in the past year, and quickly did the calculation to figure out how much that put in her pocket. She smiled to herself. Not that she could ever see herself with this guy anyway, but she had strict rules about having sex with people she dealt with on a professional basis. She did not do it. However, she would put up with flirting and verbal sparring if the client left with a smile on his face.

This one was getting exhausting though. She silently chided herself for wearing the silk white blouse and black pencil skirt she had on today. This particular top was a little more revealing than many of her business outfits, and her client could not pull his eyes away from her ample cleavage. Finally, he gave up and thanked her for all of her work. Dominique escorted him over to the exit. She gently guided him by touching his arm. She thought that was just enough to keep him happy.

Returning to her desk, Dominique sat down with a sigh. Men like that did not interest her at all. Just because they had money, they also thought they had the world's greatest cock and that they knew how to use it. When she'd dated a couple of men like that, she'd found out that it was far from the truth.

She picked up her cell phone and pressed Veronica's name. After three rings, the younger girl's voice breathlessly answered, "Hello!"

"How is your work day going, Veronica?"

"It could be better. My boss had a meeting this morning and he had me doing everything except selecting the coffee beans for the coffee. He can be such a moron. He is totally inconsiderate to us peons."

"There are some things you can do about that. We can talk about it in the future. You can have him eating out of the palm of your hand. That's more like advanced domme training. You are still learning the basics."

"I know, and I am loving it. I make so many mental notes of how I want to apply some of this in my life."

Dominique said, "I got your text last night, but it was too late to call you back when I got home. You wanted to hear about the rest of my time with Xavier?"

"Definitely. I can't get over how much you did with that man in the short time you were together. I also can not tell you how often I have become aroused thinking about your stories."

"That's a good thing. Are you up for dinner tonight? My morning has already given me a headache and I don't know what the afternoon will bring. "

"After my hellacious morning," said Veronica, "dinner sounds perfect. Where do you want to meet?"

"Remember I told you about that Italian restaurant, Ristorante La Perla of Washington, I took Xavier to? It's still there and I have a taste for pasta. Want to meet there?"

"Sounds great, Dominique. I know they have an excellent wine list."

"Deal. Dinner is on me. How about seven?"

"Works for me," said Veronica. "I'll see you there."

Dominique went back to work. She had another client review in the afternoon and had to prepare for it. She had her assistant, Travis, pull all of the paperwork together, and then she ran down the street for a quick bite of lunch. While she was waiting for her order, she had her other assistant, Jaron, call the restaurant to make the dinner reservation for her and Veronica.

The afternoon meeting went very well and Dominique did not have to fend off any advances. It may have helped that her clients were a couple in their fifties. The husband was very respectful and seemed to make a concentrated effort not to look at Dominique in any kind of sexual manner. To her amusement, though, his wife seemed to drink in her breasts, ass and legs as much as she could. Dominique had noticed that sometimes the women would check her out more than the men. She made a mental note to try to avoid ever having a meeting alone with the wife!

Before she knew it, the day wound down and Dominique made her way out of the office building. She hailed a cab and relaxed on the ride into Georgetown. She amused herself watching the movers and shakers of DC bustling about. It entertained her to see how so many of the women were so frumpily dressed, even wearing running shoes as they walked to their destinations. As the cab pulled up to the curb in front of Ristorante La Perla, she saw Veronica waiting outside the entrance. She was dressed in a rather plain, navy blue pantsuit. To Dominique, it looked like she'd got it from an old librarian line of fashion. As she paid the driver, Dominique realized that, sooner or later, she needed to take this girl out for a serious makeover,

The women embraced and went inside. The maître d' took one look at Dominique and showed her to a table in the center of the room. Dominique smiled knowingly, as she noticed this happened in almost every restaurant or bar she went into. She was always being shown off.

Dominique ordered a bottle of her favorite red wine, Estancia. She reached out to touch the lapels of Veronica's suit and ran her hand down the front. She frowned and said, "I'm guessing Rayon?" The waiter came over and uncorked their wine. After they gave their order, Veronica replied, "Honestly, I don't know, I didn't even look when I bought it." Dominique nodded and asked, "When was the last time you went clothes shopping?"

Veronica looked uncomfortable. "You don't like what I'm wearing?"

Dominique said, "It's not that. I mean, it's acceptable for work, but I want you to start realizing that being a Goddess is not just for the bedroom. It has to become a total way of life. Yes, you may tone it down at work and other places, but if you truly believe it is part of your being, then it always should be projecting, inside and out. When you look good, you feel good, which helps to raise your confidence. Hell, just by me being a confident woman exudes my power, and men know exactly what I am. Until you get to that point, though, how you dress and present yourself is a good start."

Veronica took a big gulp of wine and fidgeted in her seat. "This is something I've always had an issue with. You see, I have a big sister who is absolutely gorgeous. She does modeling and has been in music videos and other stuff like that. Growing up, she was the beauty and I was the brain. The funny thing is that our measurements are almost identical. When she comes out of the shower and sits around in her ratty old robe, we almost look like twins. When it's time to put the act on, though, she can stop traffic."

"Does she have a lot of men in her life?" asked Dominique.

"Whenever she wants," said Veronica. "However, I don't like the men she hangs around with. They are always trying to tell her what to do and boss her around. And she takes it! I guess they are the kind of guys I've always dated, but that's not what I want any more. I never liked it."

"I don't know if any woman likes it, but many are not strong enough to do anything about it."

"Like you can?"

Dominique laughed, "Absolutely. And pretty soon, you will too."

With that, their meal arrived at the table. While eating, Dominique plied the girl with questions about fashion. She tried to get an idea of what Veronica liked, where she shopped, and how she would like to dress. Dominique knew that fairly soon she would have to let her protégé feel her way around as a junior Goddess. Dominique's outlook was to always find the beauty with everything in life. It was easy to be beguiled by beautiful shiny things, but it took a discerning mind to discover the hidden harmony that leads to beauty and truth. However, Dominique knew that how a person dressed could enforce how they felt about themselves. It was important to get the shiny part down so you could see beyond that to what really mattered in a person.

Soon they were through dinner and they decided to splurge and split some tiramisu for dessert. After the waiter placed it between them, Veronica asked, "So how did your time with Xavier end?"

"It was incredible how Xavier always made me the center of his attention. He would let me know I was always on his mind. There was a text he sent me while I was at work one day that week." Dominique went into her purse and pulled out her cell. "I don't know how many phones I've been through since then, but I always made sure I kept that text." She scrolled though the phone and handed it to Veronica. "Read that."

My Goddess,

I am ready for you to arrive home, Goddess. I have your tea prepared and dinner is cooking. I am kneeling at the door and as you enter, I will lay flat on my back so that you can step on me like a doormat to wipe your shoes on. I will then carry you, my Goddess, to your throne and kneel before you. I will use my slave tongue to lick clean your beautiful boots and make sure that they are spotless. I will then remove your boots when I have cleaned them to your satisfaction. I will serve you dinner, and while you eat and watch television, I will lick clean your feet and massage them, making sure to suck each toe into my mouth and warm it with my hot breath...

Goddess, I miss you and cannot wait for you to get home so that I can call the salon and organize your pedicure!

Veronica handed the phone back to her friend. "Wow, he was really devoted to you."

"He certainly was. Xavier was terrific and I loved being with him. However, I had mixed feelings about everything during our last week together. As you know, he was the one who allowed me to be the complete Goddess I always thought I was. The day he left, he paid for my pedicure at my favorite salon, and sent me three dozen roses with a good-bye note to my office, addressed to Goddess Sasha. Part of me was sad that he would be returning to his oil rig job, because I had trained him so well. The other part of me was looking forward to being a liberated Goddess so I could continue to indulge in my new-found power. With the Goddess awakened in within me, I didn't think one man could satisfy all my deepest, darkest desires. It was all too new for me and a serious relationship wouldn't have worked at that time. I have to say, however, that we went right to the end of his stay in Washington with full force. "

Veronica had a forkful of tiramisu halfway to her mouth. In an almost pleading voice she said, "That is what I want to hear about."

Dominique smiled as she finished her last bite of dessert. She picked up her wine and said, "I'll be glad to. tell you what, though. From what I have observed so far when I tell you my stories, it's a lot safer to do it in private. Being here in the middle of everything, I really do not think people need to hear about this stuff over their lasagna. Let's get out of here and head back to my place."

"Good idea. When I start visualizing what you talk about, I may have explicit questions to ask. "

"I have another bottle of Estancia at home we can enjoy," said Dominique, as she signaled the waiter for the check. She paid it, and the two women went outside. Fortunately, a cab had just discharged two passengers right in front of the restaurant, and they hopped into it for the ride to Dominique's home.

Veronica said, "That text you showed me from Xavier was incredible. I think what gets me the most is that he really felt like that. This was not a game or a role-play with him. He was your slave."

"He certainly was," said Dominique. "That is something you will learn in time. There are guys who say they want to be your slave, but they're only pretenders. When they get tired of it, they revert back to form and try to top you from the bottom. They act like they are submissive but in reality they are not and will try to give step by step instructions on how they want you to dominate them. A true submissive will let his Goddess take control and follow her lead, waiting on her instructions. What you will discern with experience, is who is real. You've heard of 'gaydar,' where a gay person has an instinct for knowing when someone else is gay? You'll slowly develop something like that when figuring out which man has a truly subservient nature."

Veronica pondered that on the rest of the short drive to Dominique's. Once there, they got comfortable in the living room with another glass of wine. After some small talk, Veronica said, "Okay, Dominique. I'm all ears. I want to hear the rest about you and your slave.

Dominique took a sip of her wine and talked about the last days of Xavier.

****

That last week was certainly a whirlwind romance. The sex was endless. Whether it was waking up early in the morning, before bed, or in the middle of the night, I would have him take care of me. If I saw his cock even semi-hard, I would get it completely erect and he would have to fuck me. Sometimes I would wake up and find him curled up around my feet. I would prod him with a foot to wake him up and to come between my legs and feast on my pussy. He would get so hard with whatever I had him do to me. Sometimes I would fuck him, other times I would just leave him hanging until much later. He loved the ultimate tease, which was when I let him fuck me, but I would make him pull out after I came a few times, but before he did. He finally got good at preventing himself from having an orgasm.

Xavier was very adroit at keeping my shoes clean and in order. Everyday while I was at work, he would purchase a new sexy outfit for me. He especially liked the fashion shows I gave him, where I would model the clothes wearing sexy open-toed shoes. That would always lead to playtime. First, he would massage my feet and it would always lead to awesome sex. I think he washed my sheets every day because they were stained with our lovemaking.

Our last night together was on a Sunday and it was so typical of the delicious routine we'd established. That day, we finally stopped fucking long enough to get out and see some of the sights in DC. We walked around to the Capitol Building, the White House and, finally, to the Lincoln Memorial. I liked how when we were out in public, he called me "Goddess" instead of Dominique. It turned me on and showed how he wanted everybody to know that he served only me.

While we were sightseeing, my feet got tired and we decided to stop by the Teaism Restaurant and have some tea. We were sipping it and Xavier took my shoes off and massaged my feet. He didn't care that people saw him catering to me. This started to turn me on so much that I told him to hurry up and finish his tea so we could leave. We jumped in a taxicab and went back to my place.

When we got inside, Xavier did his daily ritual of stripping down naked, getting on his knees and taking off my shoes. This particular evening, he picked me up and carried me to the couch. Carefully setting me down he said, "You relax, Goddess. Leave everything to me."

With that, he went into the kitchen and reappeared carrying a cheese tray with red and green grapes. He went back, and this time he brought out a bottle of Estancia red wine and two glasses. He put on some soft music, poured me a glass of wine, and went off to the bedroom. I could smell jasmine from the candles he'd lit in there. Then I heard him running the water for a bath. I could hear other noises from there as well. He was opening packages and moving things around the room. I was very curious about what was going on in there, but I didn't move from the couch. I leaned back into the cushions with anticipation, waiting to see how Xavier was going to make our last night together a special one.

Just as I reached to pour a second glass of wine, Xavier came in and grabbed the bottle from me. He refilled my glass and poured himself one. When I was about halfway done, he stood up and took my glass from me. He extended his hand and helped me up to my feet. With a sweeping gesture, he indicated that I was to head into the bedroom.

I entered and saw that the only light was from the candles, which were flickering on the dresser and other pieces of furniture around the room. There was enough light to illuminate the red corset, garter belt, thigh high stockings on the bed and the pair of lace gloves laid out next to it. Also on the bed below the bodysuit was a pair of gold, Jimmy Choo, four-inch strappy sandals.

Before I could stop and admire these new additions to my wardrobe, Xavier led me to the bathroom where the tub was full of bubbles. He turned to face me and he slowly sunk to his knees. Reaching behind me, he unzipped my dress and helped me out of it. Very skillfully, he unhooked my bra with one hand and pulled it off. When he reached for my panties, I stopped him and shook my head. "You should know the rules. Not with your hands," I said. He knew immediately what to do and put his hands behind his back and leaned into me. He grabbed the edge of my panties with his teeth and began to pull them down, moving his head from left to right, so that I could step out of them.

He then reached out for my hand and helped me step into the tub. The water temperature was very hot, just the way I like it. I moved around in the tub to make room for Xavier, but he said, "No, Goddess, that is not necessary. I just want to please you."

I told him, "Xavier you have been a good slave. It would please your Goddess to have our last bath together."

My slave's eyes lit up like a little boy's on his birthday and he slid into the tub behind me. I could feel his muscular chest pressed up against me, as I leaned back and into his strong arms. He grabbed my sponge and then sensually proceeded to wash my entire body. He cupped his hand underneath my ass and gently rotated me to my side. I kissed his neck as his hands slid down to my feet, luxuriating in the warmth and bubbles. He spent a long time cleaning my feet. When he finished, I reached under the bubbles until I could grasp his already rock hard cock, which swelled even more in my hand. I looked Xavier in the eyes and said, "Stand up." Xavier stood and I straightened myself up. "Bring my dick closer to me, Xavier." He inched over and crouched down a bit until his massive rod was in front of me. I slowly ran my fingers over it and then cupped his balls. I never got tired of looking at it. His cock was just so big and strong. I picked up some bubbles and slathered them all over his extended member. Then I slowly started to jerk him off. I took both hands and in unison began rubbing the shaft of his cock, twisting and pulling as I went up and down, it got harder and harder. I looked at Xavier's face and he was intently looking at me with just the hint of a smile playing around the corners of his mouth. My hands started to go faster. A slight groan escaped from his lips. I pulled on him as fast as I could. His face got redder and his breathing got faster. I knew he was getting close to the edge. But before he said anything, I stopped and told him to get out of the tub. He reached into the tub to pick me up out of the water and placed me on my feet. He rubbed me with a soft bath towel until I was dry. He wrapped me in another towel and then quickly dried himself off.

Xavier's cock was still hard from the hand job I had just given him and I decided to escalate his torture with a blowjob he would never forget. Also, I couldn't resist sliding my lips down his beautiful manhood.

I didn't do the usual build up of licking softly and slowly sucking. I wanted to test his mettle, so I immediately began to suck as brutally hard as I could and even stuck a finger up his ass. I could feel his balls start to tighten. I released my mouth and went back to stroking him hard and fast. "Don't you cum without permission, slave." I began to stroke him faster and harder to see if he would be obedient and not cum. I jerked him for several minutes and loved the feeling of the friction from my hand against his raw cock. I could feel his body tense up and the veins in his dick thicken. His cock started to jump and he would try to pull it away from my vise like grip. He moaned, "Goddess, please stop. I don't want to cum without permission, Goddess. Please stop, I can't take it anymore. Oh my Goddess, I'm at the edge." The more he begged, the more intensely I squeezed his dick. I didn't let off until he stood there silently trembling with his eyes closed. This was when I knew he was right where I wanted him, so I slowly released my grip on his member. I looked with satisfaction as drops of pre-cum leaked out of his swollen tip.

Breathing hard and fast, Xavier sunk to his knees. After a couple of minutes, he calmed down and looked at me. He picked up my left hand and brought it to his lips. He gave it several soft, passionate kisses. Finally, he looked at me and said, "Thank you, my Goddess. You have brought such complete joy to my life this week. I could never have imagined my visit to DC would be this exciting."

"I've enjoyed your company too, Xavier. Now, finish getting me dressed."

He then helped me into the red corset with the garter belt and thigh high stockings and the red lace gloves. Looking in my dresser mirror, I once again thought that Xavier had excellent taste. When he sat me down and started to put on my new pair of Jimmy Choo shoes, I impulsively reached out and pulled his head between my legs. "Suck your Goddess's pussy slave," I commanded.

Xavier did just that. After all the training I'd given him, he knew exactly where to lick and suck and what I liked. It was my intention to only have him do it for a couple of minutes, but he felt so good. I reached for his head and pulled him in tighter to me. I could feel my fire grow as he worked my clit over. Finally, I couldn't hold back any longer and I came long and hard into his mouth. My legs squeezed Xavier's head like a vice, but he never complained. He just kept pleasing me until I came two more times. Overcome, I pushed him away from me onto the floor as I collapsed back on the bed. It took me a few moments to calm down. My legs would not stop shuddering from the intense spasms Xavier's mouth caused.

Eventually I stood up and straddled Xavier with a leg on each side of him. Looking down, I saw his face covered in my juices. " Slave, you have been wonderful all week. I will be sorry to see you go."

"I will be sorry to leave, Goddess. I am no further away than a phone call or a Skype connection, but I will leave it up to you, Goddess, if you want to stay in touch with this unworthy."

He was so sincere in what he said I felt a wave of affection for him. I actually was not sure what to say. I looked further down and saw his cock pointing straight up towards the opening in my corset. Maybe I didn't know what to say, but I knew what to do. "Xavier, get up off the floor and lay on your back in my bed."

He practically vaulted up and into bed with my order. I then recreated the same position on the bed as we were a moment ago on the floor, but I faced the other way. I still had my shoes on. "Slave," I said, "you are going to suck my pussy again."

I maneuvered over his face and lowered myself onto his mouth. I made sure my entire ass covered his face. I pressed into his mouth and could feel his arms wrap around my legs pulling me down. I thrust my ass and wet pussy harder into his face as he went to work licking up all of the juices that flowed out of me. I leaned slightly forward and grasped his dick with my laced covered hands. My dominance over him made him as hard as granite. Rubbing my hand over the head of his cock, I could already feel more precum dripping out of him.

I started to moan as his tongue hit the tip of my clit faster and faster. I felt my pussy start to contract again. I let go of his cock and he lifted my ass up and shoved his tongue up my asshole. My legs got weak and it felt like a bolt of electricity shot through my body. He pleasured me with his tongue just as well as he did with his fat dick. I felt so good it was like I was floating. I could hear Xavier gasping for air. I didn't think he could breathe, but since I felt a massive orgasm peaking inside of me, I didn't move. It finally hit and I yelled out as my insides forced out stream after stream of cum.

Just as I thought he was about to pass out, I got off Xavier's face. He had managed to suck in three deep breaths when I turned around and lowered myself onto his cock. I gasped as I impaled myself on his fleshy sword all the way up to the hilt. It was still a tight fit, but I was used to his dick and it was a little easier with all of the practice we'd had that week. I started to ride him as I'd never ridden anyone before.

Xavier reached out and grasped my hips to pull me in deeper and to rock my hips faster on his cock. We got into a good fuck rhythm. I would come down hard on his cock just as he thrust up with all of his strength. I took his hands and put them on my breasts. He started to massage and caress my tits and nipples. Whenever he sensed I was about to cum, he leaned forward and sucked my nipples. As I climaxed he pulled me in for a deep kiss. I moaned and could feel my pussy constrict around his dick. Juice flooded down his cock and ran down his balls. We still did not break our pace.

After my many orgasms in this position, Xavier looked at me with pleading eyes, "Goddess, may I cum?"

I leaned forward and slapped him. "No!" I screamed. "You cum when I tell you to, not before. How dare you ask!"

Xavier let out a groan of despair and closed his eyes. I started to feel him slow down. I reached under me and dug my nails into his balls. "Don't you dare. Isn't my pleasure what you live for?"

"Yes, Goddess, yes."

"Then keep fucking me until I tell you to stop." I squeezed his balls to emphasize the point. I leaned forward a little so my tits dangled in his face. "Suck my nipples, slave."

Xavier reached up and took my right nipple into his mouth. The sensation of his mouth and tongue set off another spasm from my pussy. The sound of our smacking loins coming together sounded like an audience giving us a standing ovation at Carnegie Hall . All of the lubrication from my pussy actually had me fucking Xavier faster. As he was switching his mouth from the right breast to the left, Xavier whimpered out, "Please, Goddess!"

Panting, I shouted out, "Not yet."

Tears were coming out of Xavier's eyes. It felt like his enormous cock was growing inside of me to unprecedented proportions. I was glad I was so wet. It felt like he was all the way up to my belly. I reached up and grabbed his nipple between my teeth and bit down. This made him fuck me harder. Another electric shock took over my body as I shouted out in delight. Without missing a beat he quickly flipped me over, placed me on all fours and continued to fuck me. Even though I was not on top I was still in control as I contracted my pussy muscles and squeezed his cock with every stoke inside of me. He was going deeper and deeper and I felt every inch of him going in and out. The force of his thrusting cock was becoming unbearable, but before I would tap out, I pushed my ass back on his cock and clamped down, squeezing tighter to slow him down. I focused on the feeling between my legs. I loved his cock rubbing the walls of my pussy. I tried to keep track of the tiny spasms that would grow into a massive wave that would shake my whole being. I had come so much I was in a daze. Feeling my orgasmic high, I could not believe loads of cum that this man could get out of me.

I reached behind me and cupped his balls. I massaged them and this triggered more anguished sounds from Xavier. I could feel another orgasm building in me. I could also feel his balls start to tighten. As I was about to cum, I shouted, "Now, Xavier! Now, slave, cum for me!" We both yelled so loud I'm surprised the neighbors didn't call the police. My body would not stop convulsing with the best orgasm I had that night. At the same time, Xavier exploded and he added stream after stream of his cum to the mix. It seemed like this went on for minutes. Finally, there was silence and I slumped over onto the bed.

Xavier wrapped his strong arms around me and we dozed off together that way. Sometime in the night, I woke up. I was lying comfortably in bed with the sheet around me. I looked down and saw Xavier at the foot of the bed. He had my feet outside of the covers, but he was keeping them warm by cuddling them. I smiled and moved a little to get comfortable. As I drifted back to sleep, I remember thinking that my pussy had never felt so content…and worn out… in my life!

I knew Xavier had a very early flight the next morning. He managed to get himself cleaned up and out the door without waking me. When I did wake up, I found a single red rose and a card next to my bed on the nightstand. It said how he would always treasure me and I could always call on him. He signed it by saying, "Your loving and affectionate slave, Xavier."

Chapter 8

$\mathcal{V}$eronica pushed her chair back and stretched. She looked at

Dominique with an unreadable expression on her face. Her eyes looked

magnified behind her glasses. She took a sip of her drink and finally said,

"That had to be so hard having Xavier leave like that. It certainly sounds

like you had such an intense time with him. I wish I could find a man like

that. You figured out in a week and a half what it takes most women a

lifetime to do."

Dominique nodded, "I know. I am forever thankful for him

awakening the goddess within me. I knew it was there somewhere under

the surface. I'm sure I would have gotten to the same point without him,

but it would have taken longer."

"Yeah, it was like a self-awakening on steroids!"

Dominique gave a hearty laugh. "You got that right. And I have to tell

you, that man had a dick on him that filled me up like nothing before or since. I'm not saying all my other times with men have not been good, but Xavier is in my Hall of Fame, he ranks in the top five."

A barely audible moan escaped from Veronica. "I wish I'd even had five guys that I could rank."

Dominique laughed and asked, "Do you have any vibrators? You don't have to wait for a man, you know, you can do it yourself. I need to take you shopping. There are toys we can buy that can be a big help. Plus, it is not like you only have to use them when you are alone."

Veronica looked quizzical, "What do you mean?"

Dominique explained, "Before a man can please you, you have to know how to please yourself. I've spent a lot of time exploring my sexuality. Learning exactly what I like and how I like it. I discovered all my sensitive spots and some other things I never expected, like how to squirt and contract my inner muscles to make my orgasms more powerful."

Veronica said, "Wow, I don't think I've ever experienced a real orgasm. Sure, sex feels great, but I want to learn how to make it ecstatic. So, what was it like after Xavier left? How did you go about finding guys again? Especially ones that fell into the submissive category?"

"It wasn't as hard as you would think. You have to remember, I felt incredibly free to totally be myself after Xavier. I also knew I wasn't going to settle for anything less than I really wanted in sex or a relationship. That's one thing we women do too much of. We get caught settling for a below-average man. I know you could find some good dick, but I want you to do it on your terms and with a guy you want. You're a cute woman. We could go into any bar in this city and I could help you find a man. But if it's not on your terms, where you can be the woman you want, then you are not going to enjoy it, and you'll feel like shit and even more frustrated in the morning. Do you want to just get on your back for someone, or do you want to make him lay down for you?"

Veronica took a second before answering. "I know I want to be more like you. I get a nice, warm feeling thinking what it would be like if I was telling the man what I wanted and how I wanted him to please me. Just once, I would like to keep a man hanging and not allow him to cum, instead of me not being satisfied. I would love that!"

"Don't worry, sweetie. I'll help you get to where it happens more than once. Do you know the old saying of not giving a man everything he wants at once? By being the dominant woman in the relationship, you are ramping up that old cliché. When you dominate the right man, you'll end up being satisfied like never before. He will learn that his pleasure is to be found in your pleasure."

Veronica let out a long sigh. "Yes, that is what I want. I know it. So, going back to what I asked before, what was it like after Xavier?"

"It really wasn't that difficult. I seemed to put out an aura that had the subservient type of men flocking to me." Dominique stopped for a second and then slowly nodded to herself. "I can give you a good example of the things that happened to me after Xavier left. Want to hear it?"

"Sure. You might as well get me even hornier than I already am."

Dominique laughed. "We do have to do something about that. Okay, this is what happened."

****

I was not always alone on my manhunts. I did have a partner in crime. My girl, Elizabeth but we called her Liz. Liz was a southern belle with the quintessential Dixie accent to go with it. She had soft brown hair cut into an angled bob. Liz was gorgeous and had a hot, petite shape. She had the knack for always wearing the right clothes to accentuate her figure.

Liz and I hit it off right from the very start and we got along well. She was sexy, sassy, and always had something funny to say. What I liked about her the most was that she was an aggressive flirt, just like me. When we were out partying, nobody could say we were wallflowers!

One day after work at my new firm, Liz and I decided to hang out in Old Town Alexandria. It was just a few days before her birthday and we wanted to have some adult fun. We were both on the prowl and decided to go to Union Station. It was semi-crowded for happy hour, but we saw there was a nice group of attractive men in there.

I have to say that we both caught the men's attention. Liz had on a dark blue blouse with a low cut scoop front. The black skirt she wore only came down to mid-thigh and she caught the men's eyes. As soon as she talked with that honey, southern drawl they tended to be captivated. I was no slouch that evening either. I had on a white contour dress that contrasted nicely with my skin. The dress had a deep, V neckline and I was showing some serious cleavage. As we made our way to a table, we had to be careful not to trip over the tongues that were hanging out of the guys' mouths. It didn't take long for a couple of hot ones to start up a conversation with us and buy us drinks.

They were obviously locals to that particular bar, and said that they worked for the government. Liz told them that it was her birthday and she was ready to party and have some fun. So immediately, the two men started buying shots for all of us. The bar was getting crowded and noisy. Some old-school music was playing, so Liz and I got up to dance with each other. Our breasts and asses were grinding together, which drove the men watching crazy.

As we danced, Liz kept knocking back shots. Being a good friend, I thought she might need to slow down on the drinks, so I suggested we eat dinner. The two men told us about an Irish pub around the corner that had good food. We thanked them and walked out, saying we would be back soon after we got something to eat. We wanted to leave all the men in that bar wanting more. Anticipation is an effective weapon in your arsenal of seduction. We walked to the Irish Pub, O'Donnell's and got a table right in the middle. They had a live band playing, so it was pretty packed. Here in DC, I think it's funny how many women complain about being single, because whenever I go out I notice that the men outnumber the women by about eight to one. I've never taken a poll to see who's single or married, but there are always a lot of men. O'Donnell's was no exception. My friend Liz was a talker, so it wasn't long before she'd told everyone that it was her birthday. It seemed like every guy in the place started to send over drinks.

I wasn't familiar with this area, so I didn't want to have too much to drink. I just babysat a couple of glasses, while the bar got crowded with revelers. Looking around, I noticed a group of three men. They were all very handsome and muscular. Two of them were white and one was black. He was the one that intrigued me. I immediately made eye contact with the loudest person in the group. He was wearing a blue polo shirt that showed off his chest and a nice pair of jeans that showed off his ass. He was tall with brown hair and blue eyes. He seemed confident and returned my look. He came over and asked if he and his friends could join us since we had extra space at our table. I smiled and said, "Yes." He introduced himself as Richard and his friend as John, while Leo was the black guy who had my interest. He told us they were FBI agents working at the FBI Academy in Quantico.

Richard was all over me. It was not long into our conversation when he started to touch my arm, so I quickly let him know that his actions were not welcome. I had my intentions set on Leo. Leo was quiet, but he was the one I wanted to get to know. I knew I had to gain his attention somehow. I began asking him questions about his job that successfully got him to speak up. Next, I started asking him questions about himself. He was roughly 6' 3" with smooth brown skin. He was wearing a light brown sweater that showed off his muscular chest. The short sleeves of the sweater showcased his well-developed, strong arms. I could tell he worked out hard, which I appreciated, as he looked good enough to eat.

His arms also caught Liz's fancy, as she playfully asked if she could squeeze his muscles. Richard replied, "No, but you could squeeze my muscle," as he sat back and spread his legs a little to indicate his groin. We all laughed. Richard continued to do most of the talking while Leo just smiled and laughed at his jokes. He would chime in occasionally. By now, I noticed Liz was drinking with wild abandon.

It was getting late, so we decided it was time to go. As we walked out the door Liz could barely stand, and Richard had to help her to the car. This was a huge problem because Liz was my designated driver. I knew the area where she lived, but I didn't know her exact address. In addition, we had just met these strange men and I was not sure if they were harmless, regardless of whether they were FBI or not.

When we got to the car Liz had passed out, which was no help at all. Leo started talking with his friends and came up with a quick solution. He told Richard to check Liz's purse and get her ID out, so we could see her address. Leo went over to his car, a black jaguar, and punched in her address on his GPS. He said he would lead the way to Liz's house with me as passenger, and that Richard should follow him with Liz while driving Liz's car. John would follow us because he drove Richard.

I spoke up immediately, "I am not getting into a car that my friend is not in." I did not want to be in a vulnerable position with strangers.

Leo said, "Look, we really are with the FBI." He showed me his credentials. They certainly seemed like the real McCoy. "My friends and I have greatly enjoyed your company. This is the least we can do. Besides, we are not going to jeopardize our jobs by being jerks to a couple of beautiful women."

I decided to trust him. It's not as if I had any other options, so I decided to go along with the plan.

We started driving towards Liz's house. I kept a close eye on the car behind us, making sure that Richard kept up with us. The radio was playing loud in Leo's car. It was a beautiful, black Jaguar with black leather seats, and still had that pleasant, new car aroma. We drove for about ten minutes when I noticed Richard had slowed down and pulled Liz's car over to the side of the road. I yelled at Leo to pull over. I thought that maybe Richard was trying to take advantage of Liz. I immediately jumped out of the car and ran over to the driver's side. I got in Richard's face, pointed my finger and yelled at him, "If you are trying to do something with her, I'm going to fuck you up!"

Richard pointed to the passenger side of the car. Liz was leaning out of the car and vomiting on the side of the road.

Sheepishly, I realized I had been wrong. I quickly ran around to the passenger side of the car. Both Leo and John had run to Liz's aid when we pulled over. I was glad I had found such nice guys who still helped damsels in distress.

Richard could not resist saying, "Don't worry, Dominique. I would never take advantage of Liz in this state. I want her sober so she can remember everything that we did together." He smiled and wagged his eyebrows.

All I could do was laugh at his boastfulness.

Now that I was sure Liz was okay and in such capable hands, I got back in the car with Leo and we continued the drive to Liz's home. The boys helped me get her inside and upstairs to her bedroom. I shooed them out of the bedroom, so that I could get Liz's clothes off her, and put her into bed. I tucked her in and wondered what her head was going to feel like the next morning.

I went downstairs and ushered the men out, locking the door behind me. I hugged Richard and John good-bye, and then Leo drove me to my condo. He was a perfect gentleman and his demeanor totally put me at ease. I remember the incredible night scenery from the highway as the light reflected off the water. Leo kept me interested by telling me what it was like to work for the FBI and soon we were at my home.

Leo got out, opened the door for me, and walked me to the elevator. I thought he was sweet and a bit shy. He actually seemed a little nervous. I could tell he didn't know what to do or say next. I got a kick out of how much I intimidated even a strong and powerful man like Leo. I figured behind that shyness, he would be a beast in bed.

As it came time for us to say goodbye, I leaned towards him to initiate a kiss. He then grabbed me round the waist with his right hand, firmly clasped the back of my neck with his left and pulled me closer to him. I felt the softness of his lips, the smell of his breath, and the way he rolled his tongue in my mouth. I could only imagine how he would make my pussy cum with that tongue!

As it was, I felt myself getting excited. My pussy was getting wet as he kissed me. I felt so warm, secure, and comfortable in his arms. Despite these feelings, I had to stop because I knew where it was going to go if I didn't put a halt to it, so I pressed the button for the elevator. Finally, the doors opened and I pulled back from his embrace. I smiled, said good night, and stepped into the elevator. Leo just stood there as if lightning had struck him.

I got off on my floor and walked to my door. Even before I put the key in the lock, Leo called me on my cell to make sure that I was safely inside. I thanked him for the ride home, for being a gentleman, and for that amazing kiss. I stayed on the phone with Leo until he reached his house and was in his own bed. I thanked him for getting my friend and me home safely. He thanked me for the kiss and told me that it was his pleasure taking me home because he was able to spend more time with me. It was getting late so we said goodnight and hung up the phone.

I didn't realize how turned on I was by our conversation until I clicked off the phone. I thought about things a bit. When he took control of the situation, it made me want to dominate him instead. Being wet and horny, I did what I always do in that situation. I pulled out my vibrator. My pussy was already soaking wet and I had to lay a towel on the bed under me because I knew I would be cumming a lot. I know how excited I can get. I started with my fingers rubbing my clit, and then I started fingering between my pussy lips. It felt hot and I was so wet. I put the vibrator on my clit and set it to the highest setting. I thought about Leo, and how he'd made me feel that evening. I pressed the vibrator between my legs, while my fingers started to massage the inside of my soft wet folds. I got more excited when I thought about how shy Leo was and how I could break him out of his shell. I could not wait to see what exciting things he would like to do with me, or what I could do to him. I had multiple orgasms until I fell into a deep, relaxing sleep.

The next morning I received a text from Leo asking me if I had any plans for Saturday. Since I wasn't busy I replied that I would love to see him, so we made plans to see each other then.

On Saturday, I wanted to wear something sexy, but chic and classy. I wore my white silk dress that hugged my curves and a pair of red, strap sandals that showed off my new pedicure. I let my hair down, and put on a little make-up and shiny lip-gloss. The final touch was some erotic perfume and I was ready to go.

Leo came early, so it was a good thing that I was ready. He called and said he was outside waiting. When I came downstairs, I could immediately tell from his expression that he definitely approved of what I was wearing.

He was standing next to his lovely car and opened the door for me. As I got closer, he said, "You sure look beautiful. Wow!"

"Thank you, Leo. I am glad you like. I'm looking forward to seeing what the day has in store for us."

We headed for brunch at Sequoia's. It was a beautiful, sunny day, the temperature was perfect and there was a gentle, warm breeze. When we arrived, I was pleasantly surprised. The place was very upscale with long, white tablecloths and soft, romantic music playing. I have always loved the water, so we sat on the patio near the river.

The restaurant had everything set up for royalty, and everyone was dressed to the nines. We sat down, ordered Mimosas, and made small talk while we waited for our food. After the conversation and meal, we went to the Kennedy Center to enjoy a play. We spent the whole day together, laughing, joking and having fun.

As we walked from the Kennedy Center to the car, Leo shyly pressed his hand into mine. He subtly intertwined our fingers together and I felt his strong grip. All I could think about was how perfect his hands would be for massaging my feet.

I asked, "Did Richard and Liz ever hook up?"

Leo said, "No, it didn't work out."

"I do want to thank you again for being such a gentleman the other night. I appreciate you getting both us girls home safely."

Leo shyly nodded his head in acknowledgement. So far, this day had been way too vanilla for my taste. I knew what I wanted. I wanted him to embrace me as he had the last time I saw him. I longed for him to touch me and to feel his dick deep inside me. From the look in his eye, I knew he wanted this too, but he was trying to keep himself under control. I decided to play along, just to tease him.

I could tell he was nervous again and did not know what to do. He probably didn't want to make a mistake. I knew there was a fire burning inside of him that needed release. His inner animal was begging to come out, and I just had to find a way to bring it to the surface.

It was time to take me home and he opened the door of the car for me again. We drove the long way to my house. I really liked talking with him and hearing about his exciting job with the FBI, but I didn't quite understand why he was being so shy and withdrawn. Normally, I couldn't keep a man from trying to touch me. Leo was different, though, and I was interested to see what he would do when he got me home.

We got out of the car and he walked me to the elevator. Once again, I did not invite him up because I wanted him to initiate things. I was beginning to wonder how long it would take him to make a move. We stood there waiting for the elevator when he asked, "Could I come up to use the bathroom?" I laughed at his question and invited him up.

However, he was not that innocent once we got on the elevator. He gave me a sweet, soft kiss on the lips. The cologne he was wearing was one I had not smelled before, and the aroma instantly aroused me. I pushed Leo up against the wall and rolled my tongue deep inside his mouth. He grabbed me with both arms and hugged me tightly. The sensation of my soft, round breasts pressing up against his firm chest started my pussy gushing. We were so much into each other that we didn't realize we had missed the elevator stopping on my floor. I knew this was the night that I would have him, but I wanted to hear him beg first.

We spent so much time going up and down in the elevator that I thought we might not ever get out. We didn't let go of each other until we got back to my floor. As he stood at my door fumbling with my keys, I couldn't wait to get him alone. I was curious to see what he was working with.

Once we got inside my condo, I fetched a bottle of red wine and two glasses to help ease away his nervousness. I put on some soft music and sat down very close to Leo with my legs touching his. My dress showed off my ample cleavage and enough of my legs to drive him crazy.

We finished the bottle of wine, but Leo still did not make a move! I decided to take matters into my own hands and turn up the heat a little with a kiss. He held my head and pulled me close to him. I felt the firmness of his chest and I rubbed my hand across his pants to see how firm he was there. To my surprise, he was not even hard! I was disappointed and perplexed.

Leo noticed that I was drawing back from him. He did not know what to do, but I did. As he pulled back and asked to go to the bathroom, I immediately grabbed him and forced him back down on the couch. I straddled him and kissed him passionately, hoping to get a rise out of him. I sensed his excitement and paused just for a slight second to remove my shoes. As I started to unbuckle my strap sandals, he grabbed my hand and said pleadingly, "Please don't take them off."

Finally, I could see a large bulge in his pants. I suddenly realized that he was hard because he liked my feet. Leo also had a foot fetish.

I decided to have some fun. "So you don't want me to take my shoes off? Then get on your knees and beg me not to."

He immediately dropped to his knees and began to kiss my toes. He said, "Dominique, please don't take off your shoes. You look so sexy and I love the way your beautiful feet look in these shoes. I would do anything for you." He looked up into my eyes. "What do you want me to do?"

I spread my legs open and slowly guided Leo's head between them. He looked up at me with a smile and put his head into my pussy. He began to suck my clit gently, which made me cum. I was so excited that I opened my legs even wider. I lifted myself slightly off the couch and pushed myself into his face. I then wrapped my legs around his neck with my high heels digging into his back. He wrapped his arms underneath my thighs and lifted me up to bury his face deeper inside me. He began to lick my black cat more intensely and hit all the right spots. With his face still buried in my pussy, he picked me up with his strong arms and carried me to the bedroom. I knew what he wanted next, but I wanted to be in control, so I stopped him.

He looked confused and asked, "Is everything okay?"

I replied, "Yes, everything is just fine, but now it's my turn." I stood up and started to unzip his pants. Finally, I could see what was down there. He was wearing a thin pair of boxers and everything showed through it. I was very pleased with the package.

Leo was so excited that he could not wait, and he tried to help me take his pants off. I stopped him and said, "No, I don't need any help. I know what I'm doing."

He stopped and stared into my eyes like an animal that had been starving for weeks. Now that he had a juicy piece of meat sitting in front of him, though, he could not even get a taste. Leo started breathing harder. Then with both hands, I grabbed the top of his pants and pulled them down in such a way that my breasts brushed against his cock. When I did that, his dick got even harder and that got me even more excited. I was happy that I could so easily get him to this point. However, I wanted to see how much further I could take him.

I knew he had a foot fetish, but I wondered if he knew. He stepped out of his pants and I pushed him back on the bed. He was lying on his back looking up at me helpless. I began to take off my clothes, first my dress and then bent over to take off my shoes. He quickly sat up to ask if he could be of any assistance. I stopped and said, "Yes, take them off for me."

He obeyed and once they were off, he tried to kiss my pedicured toes. I kicked him lightly in the face as a warning and told him, "I didn't give you permission to do that." He stood up and I quickly pushed him down on the bed again. I put my finger over his mouth. I admonished him, "Be quiet and I don't want to say it again." He nodded his head guiltily.

I then directed him to take off his shorts, which he immediately ripped off. I stood over him on the bed with my hands on my waist in a dominating pose. This got him very excited again, and he instinctively grabbed my calves. To show him I was the boss, I kicked his hands off me. I pointed my toes at his head in an accusing manner and told him, "Do not touch me again unless I tell you to."

Like a well-trained boy, he said, "Yes, Dominique."

At this, I said, "And from now on, you are to address me as Goddess."

"Yes, Goddess."

I rewarded him for his obedience by rubbing my foot all over his face. He opened his mouth so that he could lick my feet. Instead, I lifted his chin with my foot and closed his mouth.   "You silly foot slut. Did I tell you to open your mouth? I just wanted you to smell my feet and see how they feel. You don't deserve to lick them yet."

I could see the desperation and disappointment in his eyes. I had him right where I wanted him. "Sit up," I commanded. By now I was sitting at the opposite end of the bed facing him, and I angled my feet so I could squeeze his dick between them. I began to rub my feet up and down on the shaft of his hard cock. His head went back and he began to moan louder. The louder he moaned, the faster I massaged his dick with my feet. I could tell he was getting close to exploding, so I stopped. I liked the idea of bringing him up and down on a sexual roller coaster.

I lay down on my back and told him to massage me. He started working my pussy with his finger. He asked, "May I use my mouth on your beautiful pussy?"

In reply, I grabbed his head and forced it down there. I was so ready that as soon as his tongue touched my clit, my cum squirted on his face. He was shocked for a second, then recuperated and buried his face fully into my pussy.

Leo eventually came up for air and begged, "Goddess, can I please feel?"

I laughed at how he put that and teased him "You are feeling me right now."

He said, "No, I want to feel inside you."

I asked, "If I let you slide your dick in my pussy what would you do?"

He replied in a defeated whisper, "Whatever you want me to."

I lifted his face up to mine with one hand, and with the other, I guided his cock to my pussy. He put his dick in the opening and he tried to force himself inside of me, but I was too tight. He was so excited with just his tip inside me that he came right then and there. I could see he was disappointed, and it almost looked like he was going to cry as he said, "Sorry."

I gave him a stern look and said, "Yes, I know you are very sorry."

Little did he know that it was his first and last chance with me. I walked him to the door, told him goodnight and never bothered to call him again.

****

Dominique looked up and saw Veronica hanging on her every word. Her breathing was hard and ragged, and she looked like she wanted to jump out of her skin.

"So you see, Veronica," said Dominique, "the lessons I learned with

Xavier served me well with other men. I could tell fairly quickly that Leo had a foot fetish. It did not take a whole lot of manipulation to turn that into my advantage."

Veronica took a deep breath and fanned herself with her hand. "So once I get the hang of this, it becomes more automatic?"

"It becomes part of you, dear. That's the point we want to get you to."

With that, Dominique picked up her glass and held it out to the young woman. Veronica picked up hers and together they clinked rims. They smiled at each other in understanding of the heights Dominique would help Veronica attain.

Chapter 9

*T*he following Friday, Dominique and Veronica agreed to meet after work for Happy Hour at an Irish Pub called Four Courts. Dominique sat at her desk and reflected on the good week she'd had at her office. Being part of one of the top-rated financial companies in Washington, D.C. kept her busy, and she was getting better at her job every day. *Barron's,* America's premier financial magazine, backed up her company's status in their annual rating of financial institutions.

She had started out here like her new friend, Veronica, at her office. It had taken a lot of work, but now Dominique was one of the thirty-two advisors working here. Out of that thirty-two, only four were women and besides herself, the only other black person in such a lofty position was a man who could give a jellyfish a run on who had more of a backbone.

Looking at the time, she decided to call it a week. She called in Jaron and Travis, her assistants. They were both, young, bright, and good at their jobs. They treated Dominique like a Goddess, though in a much sweeter and fawning way than any man she had dated in her life. If the office policies had allowed it, they would have placed a throne behind her desk for Dominique to sit on. They did their work well, and were outstanding as her palace guards in screening people and setting up appointments for Dominique. When warranted, they could also run interference for her when her bosses were being a pain in the ass.

Jaron came in first. He was tall, skinny, blond, and wearing a pair of gray slacks with a crisp, pink shirt and a pale blue tie. He was in his mid-twenties, but looked like he should still be in prep school. He was a product of that environment, graduating from Princeton and starting at an entry-level position as he made his way up the financial services ladder. One night, Dominique had taken Jaron and Travis to dinner. It was there that Jaron had said that his father had been grooming him to join the family business. Jaron found he then had to make his own way in the world. The kid was doing great and Dominique thought he was learning very well.

"Travis will be here in a minute, Dominique. He's putting away the last of the review documents from today."

"That's fine," said Dominique. "I just wanted to tell you two to get out of here. Enjoy the weekend and don't think about this place until Monday."

"I like how that sounds. We did an awful lot this week," said Jaron.

Dominique thought back over the week. Aside from her time with Veronica, it had been all work. Here at the company, she met with clients and advised them on their finances. This involved detailed financial planning that meant creating budgets, advising on investments (stocks, annuities, mutual funds), managing retirement accounts, and conducting estate planning. To accomplish this, she first had to interview clients to determine their current income, expenses, insurance coverage, tax status, financial objectives, risk tolerance, and other pertinent information. When she had as much data as she could gather, Dominique could then recommend strategies on debt management, cash management, insurance coverage, and investments.

While she was working with clients, she also had to identify and keep abreast of new market trends in the industry. Travis and Jaron had been with her for a year now and they were a big help to her in every aspect of her job. Dominique was skilled in delegating the tasks that they could handle while performing the work that only she could do. The three of them had been a team for a year now, and her little area of the company was the best in terms of organization and client satisfaction.

As Dominique finished reflecting on what the two young men did for her, Travis scampered into her office. Travis was about the same age as Jaron but there their similarities ended there. Travis was shorter and a little stouter, with the dark hair and complexion of his Hispanic heritage. Today he was wearing tan Chinos and a navy blue sweater. He had grown up in the intercity of Atlanta. In spite of the odds, he focused on his studies in high school and went to a local community college for two years. His outstanding grades enabled him to complete his last two years on scholarship at Georgia Tech and this job brought him to Washington. He was always smiling, and was now a little out of breath as he said, "Jaron told me you wanted to see us. What's up?"

"I was just telling Jaron that you two are done for the week. Good job on everything I gave you to do. It would be difficult to do this without you."

"We wouldn't want to work for anyone else here but you, Dominique," said Travis.

"That's right," said Jaron. "Everybody else here can be such a stick in the mud. According to most of the other assistants, their bosses yell at them all the time."

"My belief is that you treat people like you want to be treated. So, are you two doing anything fun this weekend?"

"We both have papers due this week," said Jaron. Both young men were enrolled in a Master's program at George Washington University. "But tonight I promised Travis I'd be his wingman at that bar over on U Street."

"Well, be careful out there. This town can be strange. See you Monday, guys."

"Goodnight, Dominique," they said in unison and left her office.

Dominique took a few more minutes to put the files away that she had been looking at. Standing up, she stretched and looked out her window. Spring was making everything bloom and it was so nice to see the blossoms and leaves popping out after such a long winter. Today she had worn a simple, cream Armani jacket and skirt with a light pink shirt. She picked up the jacket from the client chair in front of her desk, put it on, and left her office, locking her door behind her.

She joined the stream of her colleagues making their way out of the office building. Everybody was preparing to celebrate TGIF in their own way. Dominique found herself looking forward to having a drink and chatting with Veronica. She enjoyed the younger woman's company and found herself constantly thinking of what she needed to do to prepare the girl to become a Goddess. Descending in the elevator Dominique found herself thinking, "I really need to get her spruced up. She has a nice figure, and I think she has a nice set of boobs under that stuff she calls a wardrobe. I just have to make time to take her shopping."

Dominique turned when she hit the sidewalk and headed for the place where she and Veronica first met. The walk was easy and Dominique was well aware of the glances she received from men and women alike. It was not just her looks and the well-tailored clothing that caught people's attention. It was the way she carried herself. In another place and another time, onlookers would have taken her for royalty.

When Dominique entered the bar, she quickly scanned the area for Veronica. It did not appear that she was there yet. Dominique spied the same table they had sat at before. Someone was just leaving it. She sped over and took command of the table before anyone else grabbed it. Friday evening and Happy Hour meant that the place was packed. She ordered a glass of wine when the waitress came over. She sat back and waited for Veronica.

Dominique was idly reading the appetizer menu when a large, black man stylishly dressed in a sharp-looking suit came over to the table. "Well, little lady, it looks like you can use a little company."

Her eyebrows arched slightly at the "little lady" line. Dominique sighed and said sweetly, "Well, do tell. And what do you have in mind?"

The man started to pull out the other chair. "I was thinking I'd buy you a drink and we could talk for a bit. I'm visiting here in town and looking for a dinner companion. I thought if I take you to dinner, then you can show me the sites of your lovely city. I'm sure that if you show me what looks good at night here, I can show you how Max makes all the women smile back home."

Dominique hated guys like this. There were alpha males, and then there were pretend alpha males. This blowhard fell in the latter category. "Max, do all the women smile back home because your dick is so little?" asked Dominique in a friendly voice.

Max was taken aback. He stopped trying to maneuver into the chair. He started spluttering, "No, not at all…"

"I suppose," said Dominique, "that there is a Mrs. Max in the picture too. Right?"

Max went from acting annoyed to sheepish in about a half a second.

"Well, ah, I mean…"

"Do me a favor, Max. Just take your married ass and get out of here before this gets ugly."

Max looked at Dominique for a second and decided prudence was the wise move. He let go of the chair and said, "Sorry." He spun away as if Dominique was radioactive.

As his bulk headed back to the bar, Veronica appeared. She must have been standing right behind him. "I see you are doing your part to keep the jerks in town in line," she said with a big smile.

"Technically, he was a visiting jerk. How much of that did you see?"

"I got to the table the same time he did. Since he could cause a solar eclipse by himself, I don't think you were able to see me. "

"He was a big boy," said Dominique. "Did you enjoy the show?"

Veronica sat herself on the vacant chair. "Very much. You were great. I think that's the first time I've smiled all day."

Dominique signaled the waitress. When she got to their table, Veronica gave her order. Then Dominique asked, "Did you have a bad day today?"

"I hate to say this," Veronica said as she nodded, "but every day there is bad. Most of the people there are nice, but the guy I directly work for is such an ass. He thinks he knows everything. He's a male chauvinist and thinks he can work me harder than a Hebrew slave. That's how he usually is, but today I think he tried to grab my ass. That was a first, even for him."

Dominique had noticed that Veronica had on tight, black slacks and a blue top. If the guy was a dope, then the slacks were as good as painting a bull's eye on her ass. She asked, "You know you can file a complaint against him."

"Yeah, but there were no witnesses and it would be my word against his. You know how that goes."

Dominique said, "I know. It's a losing proposition."

"Have you dealt with that in work?"

"I guess when I was starting out like you, I did a little. I didn't let it get very far, though."

"How do you handle it?"

"Tell you what. I'm ready for another glass of wine. Why don't we order some appetizers to share and I'll give you some of my techniques for dealing with stuff like that."

"Great idea. I'm hungry too. And any advice you can give me would be appreciated."

The two women talked over what appetizers to order. The waitress came back, took their order, and said she'd be back with drink refills for both of them plus their food in a few minutes.

Dominique and Veronica talked about what they were going to do over the weekend. When their order arrived, they dove into the appetizers. After a couple of minutes, Veronica sat back and said, "OK, so how do you deal with assholes in the office?"

"Well, as you know, assholes come in all categories. They can be your peers, subordinates, and bosses. Let me tell you a little about how I handle my boss. I think that is the pertinent lesson for tonight."

Dominique took a sip of wine and dabbed her mouth with her napkin as she got her thoughts in order. Then she began. "My boss is Marcus Jordan. I have been at my place for eight years now. Marcus was the guy who hired me and he's a nice-looking dude. He's, like, six foot one, and two hundred and twenty pounds. I think he played football in college and is still pretty fit. I know he goes to the gym. When I was looking for a gym to join, I asked him where he went. Then I made sure to join a different one!"

Veronica laughed, "Yeah, I don't think I want my boss to see me in my workout clothes."

"As a rule of thumb," said Dominique, "always try to keep your professional and personal life separate. It makes life so much easier. Never, ever fuck your boss. If you do, you better start polishing up your resume."

"Ok, I'll remember that," said Veronica.

"Now, Marcus is married with two kids. He has a boy and a girl and he loves being a father. He often arranges his schedule so that he can be at soccer games or school events. Marcus is about twenty years older than I am, but when I met his wife, I figured she was only about five years older than me. So I knew the dude was into younger women. She is a very nice lady by the way."

"He sounds a little more well-rounded than my boss. He is thirty and obnoxious."

"Marcus is not obnoxious. He is a charming and a smart man. I think he graduated in the top ten of his class. He also has a great sense of humor. He can make me laugh. When I think of Marcus, I think of the Alpha Male."

"Alpha Male?" asked Veronica.

"Yes. I was just thinking about this when old Max tried to seduce me in his quiet way." Dominique smiled at her joke. "I thought how Max was pretending he was an alpha male, but he was purely delusional. A real Alpha Male commands respect from people. His abilities to lead and be in charge are based on his personality and accomplishments. Unless he is a complete moron, an Alpha Male should be in charge. You know, Xavier, was very much an Alpha Male. I could see him in charge of his oilrig without a problem. With me, he chose to let his subservient side out because I was the kind of woman who wanted to bring it out. Just so you know, an Alpha Male does not necessarily have to be like that in every aspect of his life. I have known some Alphas who were so tired of being in charge all the time, they looked forward to their time in the bedroom to finally give up control for a while."

Veronica asked, "These are the guys that you explained to me are only pretend subs? They can turn it on and off? "

"That's right. You see, Xavier was a pure sub for his Goddess. I think that is what you would eventually like to find."

"I think so too. Tell me more about Marcus."

"Marcus is a hard ass. I remember my interview and the way he explained the job. He talked about how stressful the position was. He said, 'If you don't work hard you don't eat.' In other words, if you don't hustle, you won't make any money. My relationship with Marcus is a unique one. In the beginning, we did not get along very well. Before he became the executive office manager, he was my direct supervisor. He was my mentor who was supposed to teach me how to interview clients, and get them to believe in me enough to trust me to handle their money."

"I get the same speeches where I am," said Veronica.

"I heard it constantly. Now, Marcus is a man who is very aware of him self. Everything he does is calculated. While training me he would constantly ask me questions. For example, many times he would assign me something to do and I'd get in the groove of doing it, only to find that all of a sudden, he'd call me into his office to explain to him how to do things on his computer. This seriously frustrated me because I thought he should be the one showing me how to do things."

"He didn't know how to use his computer?" asked Veronica.

"He damn well did know how to use his computer," exclaimed Dominique. "He'd been with the company for twenty years at this point. This went on for weeks. One day my co-worker, Jonathan Arnold, sensed my frustration and anger with Marcus. Jonathon and I had started at the same time, and he invited me to accompany him to lunch. I explained to him why I was so pissed off. I thought Marcus was testing me, or that he was trying to get me to quit. If Marcus was trying to bring out the bitch in me, I wanted to know why."

Veronica finished her plate of appetizers and asked, "Did Jonathon offer any insight?"

"He laughed and smiled at me and said, 'No, the last thing Marcus wants you to do is quit. He knows what he's doing. He calls on you a lot because he likes being close to you. He uses the dumb act as an excuse to get you into his office and next to him.'"

"You didn't pick up on that?"

"No, Veronica, I look back and laugh at how naïve I was back then about some things. I realized that I was flattered he felt like that but then I started to get mad, as it was not his place to force me to be close to him."

"Besides, your philosophy of not screwing around with the boss comes into play," said Veronica.

"That is very true. I was still putting my own code of conduct at work together in my head, but I had worked hard to get into that company and I took my role seriously. I was naïve about some things, but I instinctively knew that I could not afford to compromise myself by dating someone I worked with. If the relationship went well, it could be a distraction. However, if the relationship went south, that would add all kinds of unnecessary drama at work. Throw in the fact that he was married and my boss, and there were no positives at all. I also knew I was not going to give any man that much control over me."

"Did you think about reporting him?"

Dominique nodded, "Initially, I thought about reporting him to human resources for sexual harassment, but I decided on a different tact. That very afternoon before I went back to work, I freshened up my make-up, put more perfume on, and even rubbed some all over my exposed skin. I had perfume all over my body. I also unbuttoned an extra button on my blouse. Then I deliberately returned from lunch fifteen minutes late. As I knew he would, Marcus called me into his office. I sat down in front of his desk and he started out by asking, 'Did you know you were late?' I looked at him directly in the eye and replied, 'Yes' without cracking a smile. Marcus asked, 'Dominique, are you ok? Is there something I can help you with?'"

"You certainly put him on the defensive," said Veronica.

"I certainly did," agreed Dominique. "I had him a little discombobulated and his face started to turn red. Then I got up and walked behind the desk to where he was sitting. I stood over him and began to talk about one of the clients I was assisting before I went to lunch. Marcus quickly turned in his chair to face me. I was standing there and could see that his legs were wide open. I took a quick glance down and noticed an erection in his pants. I stepped in closer. It was just enough to barely touch him. I could sense that he was going to try to make his move, but before he did, I kicked his legs closed and apologized for touching him. Then I leaned over him to pull up the client's name on the computer."

Veronica was smiling at the antics in the story. She asked, "How did Marcus handle that?"

"I heard Marcus sigh deeply. I swung my head around so I was looking him in the eye again and asked him if everything was OK. He just shook his head, speechless. With that, I excused myself and went back to my office. Now that I was onto his game, anytime he tried his shit with me, I nonchalantly got in his face like that. It wasn't long before he stopped his nonsense."

"Did things get better or worse when he realized you were on to him?"

"Things got much better. He began to respect me more and left me alone to do my job. Eventually, he gave me more responsibility and sent new clients my way. Marcus began to realize what an asset I was. I was unlike any other financial adviser in the office or in the DMV area. I was a very attractive woman who was intelligent and knew how to apply my smarts to the job. I was a quick learner about this business and could quickly earn my client's trust.

"As I said Marcus was smart. He observed what I was doing and knew how well that I did my job. He kept encouraging me and I was building up a big book of business. It was not long before I was advising him on what to do. Soon, the owners and partners of the company noticed the increase in clients and revenue that I was bringing in under Marcus's supervision. They gave him a promotion and I continued to thrive."

"What's your relationship like now?" asked Veronica.

"We are actually very close. He knows his boundaries. He talks to me a lot about his kids and his wife. Sometimes, I flirt with him just enough to get what I want. This drives him crazy, but the teasing empowers me. Whenever he gets it into his head that I am actually about to do something with him, I just bring up his wife and kids in a conversation and tell Marcus how much I admire him because he loves them so much. It's like throwing ice water on his balls."

Veronica let out a loud laugh. "I love it. So that is how you tamed him? Turned the flirting thing around onto him?"

"Pretty much," said Dominique. "Have you ever heard the saying that the best way to deal with a bully is to punch him in the nose?"

Veronica nodded.

"Dealing with asshole men is pretty much the same. They think they are all of that and a bag of chips, but when you are the one to get aggressive, they don't know what to do. They aren't used to it. If they think you are their equal or even stronger than them, they cave."

"What if a man doesn't back down?"

"Then you do what I did with Marcus. If I had given him an opening, he would have jumped on me faster than a flea onto a dog. But I never gave him that chance. I established boundaries about what I would do and never went over the line. In the workplace, you have to add one caveat. You have to work your ass off and produce. Then nobody can touch you."

Looking thoughtful, Veronica spun her empty wineglass around in her hand. "I'm not sure if I can pull that off."

"You have to have a Goddess mindset. While it means one thing in your sex life, you also need to channel that attitude into the other parts of your life. I think we can get you there with a little more work. I know you have the desire. We are going to start channeling that into action."

"How?"

"You've been listening to enough of my stories and how I go about things at this point. I think a little shopping is in order. What do you think about having a makeover?"

"You mean my clothes."

"Clothes, make-up, perfume, manicure, pedicure…the works. Do you always wear those glasses?"

"I did wear contacts. I've been putting off buying some new ones."

"It's time to start doing, sweetie. Order some new contacts. Let me know when you get them and we'll hit the stores. I want to do this when you aren't wearing glasses. I already think you're a pretty girl, but we are going to make you smoking hot!"

"Nobody ever called me hot," stated Veronica.

"That's why the makeover. When you look hot, you feel hot, and, damn it, you are hot. Before that, I want you to do two things."

"What's that?"

"When you go back to the office on Monday, stop taking grief from your boss. Until we get you looking your best so you can use all of your assets, do not put up with anything out of line from him. Be respectful, but firm. And until we get you some new outfits, do not wear tight pants to the office anymore. I'm looking at your ass in the pants and I want to touch it. Those things are begging for a guy to touch your ass. I'll show you how to use that to your advantage, but not in work. Not yet anyway."

"That sounds good," said Veronica. "What's the other thing?"

"We are going shopping tomorrow. I need to help you buy and get familiar with some toys that will help with your Goddess training. I want you to be ready when you finally come out of your shell. So come to my place at noon tomorrow. We are going to a pleasure store."

Chapter 10

*P*romptly at twelve the next day, Dominique heard a knock on her door. She opened it to find a smiling Veronica decked out in tight jeans, a light blue sleeveless blouse, and holding a windbreaker over her left arm. A pair of ankle boots added another inch to her height. She had on a pair of sunglasses and her hair curled up at her shoulders. She looked fresh-faced and ready for anything.

"Come on in," said Dominique. "Let me get my coat."

"You just need something light," said Veronica. "It's pretty warm out today and the sun is shining. It's a beautiful day not to be working. And you are looking as gorgeous as ever."

Dominique smiled at the compliment. She had on a lavender, button-down blouse and black skirt. She wore a stunning pair of black sandals, which were also incredibly comfortable for wandering through the shops. She had visited the beauty salon earlier in the morning so that her manicure and pedicure matched her shirt. A simple necklace and earrings rounded off the ensemble.

As Dominique looked around in the hall closet for a suitable jacket she asked, "You are inside you know. You can take off the sunglasses."

"Not yet. I managed to get an early morning appointment with my optometrist. She put those drops in my eyes to get them to dilate and they are still bothering me without the glasses. I took your advice about getting contacts again. Unfortunately, I had to go through the whole exam thing since it has been a couple of years. I can pick up my contacts in a couple of days."

Dominique was pleased that Veronica had reacted to her suggestion so quickly. It was a pleasure to teach someone who had the hunger to learn. This afternoon should be fun. Dominique chose a coat, and the two women went outside and signaled a cab to stop and pick them up.

Inside the cab, Dominique instructed the driver to go to _Le Tache Couples Boutique on King Street in Alexandria. Nestling back into the seat, she asked Veronica, "Have you ever been in a store like the one we're going to?"

"I did once with my first boyfriend. It was just kind of a goofy thing. I was only eighteen at the time. We never did buy anything. I have a dildo and a vibrator at home, but I ordered them online. By the way, I don't think I've ever used them as often as I have in the past couple of weeks listening to your adventures. Your tales are more erotic than any stories I have ever read or any porn I've watched."

Dominique explained, "Real life can be a hell of a lot more exciting if you do it right. For a woman to reach those heights, it usually means you have to be in control of the situation. Unless your man is very enlightened sex is usually five minutes of foreplay, he fucks you, cums, and then turns over and goes to sleep. You're with a guy but you find yourself reaching for your toys for satisfaction instead of the man snoring next to you."

"That pretty much sums up my experience," said Veronica. "I'm going to change that. I'm nervous about this, but I am determined."

"Good girl!" said Dominique. "Look at it this way. Have you given a presentation at college or work?"

The girl nodded. "Actually, quite a few."

"Remember how nervous you were the first time? Then they got a little easier each time you had to do another one. Working your way up to being a cherished Goddess is a lot like that. It may seem a little artificial and you will feel like you are acting in the beginning. As you do it more and more, it will become natural to you. Practice, practice, practice…and I cannot think of anything more fun to practice at!" Dominique laughed and Veronica joined in.

Dominique continued, "The place we are going is a bit more upscale than your average sex store. I want you to look around and see what you are comfortable using and wearing."

"Wearing?" asked Veronica.

"Yes, you should get one or two outfits so you are ready when your first opportunity with a sub occurs. Men are extremely visual. I swear I have been with a couple of men who were ready to cum as soon as they saw me dressed as their ultimate fantasy. They needed a lot of training in terms of premature ejaculation."

As she finished talking, the cab stopped. Dominique reached for her pocketbook, but Veronica said, "I got this." She handed some bills to the driver. He looked at them with his eyes wide, a red face, and seemed slightly out of breath. Dominique smiled in amusement when she realized the driver understood English and had heard their conversation.

Together, they entered the store. It was a great deal bigger than Veronica thought it would be. The right side of the store displayed many different clothes, lingerie, and other apparel items. On the left were rows of shelves and racks holding many different types of toys and devices. Veronica was happy that she had an expert with her. She would have been overwhelmed and embarrassed if she'd come here for the first time by herself.

Dominique headed over to the clothes. "Let's find something that you like and makes you look hotter than you've ever been!"

The women went up and down the aisles and took turns pulling out different combinations of outfits. After a lot of sorting and discussion, Veronica took a few items to the fitting rooms at the back, with Dominique trailing her. She went into one of the large booths and shut the doors behind her. She stripped out of her top and bra, and peeled her jeans and panties off.

First, she put on the black items. They were cut like sexy, summer PJs, with a brief pair of shorts and a sleeveless top. Unlike any PJs Veronica had ever worn before, this outfit was totally see-through. She liked black and thought this might be a good first choice. She looked in the mirror and liked what she saw. It looked extremely sexy on her figure without being slutty. "Hey, Dominique," she called out. "Is anyone out there?"

"No, why?"

Veronica opened the door. "Because I want your opinion."

Dominique took in the girl standing slightly back from the doorway in the changing room. She had been correct in thinking Veronica had a hot body hiding under her current wardrobe. She analytically looked over the girl's body. Veronica had a very nice set of breasts that stood almost straight out with nice nipples. They appeared hard and prominent from the coolness in the store. Dominique narrowed her eyes and decided they were the real thing, and the firmness was the product of youth and good genes.

The outfit looked dynamite on the girl. From their conversations

Dominique knew Veronica went to the gym, and her toned abs, arms, and legs showed that she used her time wisely there. Glancing down, Dominique noticed that her pussy was shaved with the exception of a small tuft of dark hair right around the slit. Making a spinning motion with her finger, Dominique had the girl turn around. Veronica did so and treated Dominique to a view of a muscular back, firm legs, and an incredibly sexy, round fat ass. No wonder her boss copped a feel!

Dominique said, "That suits you fine. How do you feel in it?"

"Very sexy. I could see myself surprising a man while wearing this." She closed the door and tried on a different outfit. This one was a light-gold lace body suit. The translucent material attached to her wrists and ankles with elastic. It covered her completely with the exception of an opening around her pussy. As she looked in the mirror, Veronica started to feel herself getting moist at what she saw. She thought she looked terrific, sexy, and sensual. Before meeting Dominique, she would never have even thought of dressing like this.

She pulled open the door and said to Dominique, "How about this one?" To her horror, Dominique was talking with a tall, statuesque blond that had some things she was bringing to the fitting room. She'd half-closed the door again when Dominique called out, "It's OK. This is Missy. She's a friend of mine and we have partied together a few times. Let us see you."

Veronica widened the door again. The other women looked her up and down. Dominique nodded in approval. Missy said, "Very sweet and sexy." She licked her lips. "You look good enough to eat. And I mean that!"

Veronica gave an uneasy chuckle and went back inside. She undressed and felt like her pussy was about to gush right there in the changing room. She had never had sex with a woman before in her life, but Missy's attention made her excited. Oh well, something else she would have to figure out later.

She gathered up the two outfits and exited the fitting room. "I am going to get these," she announced to Dominique.

"Great choices. By the way, now that I've seen your body, our next shopping expedition is going to be for that total makeover. You have a great body, sweetie. The way you dress, though, is like keeping a Corvette hidden in the garage. It should be out motoring around so that everyone can admire it."

Veronica felt herself blush a little as they headed over to the toys. She was beginning to wish she had not put on such tight pants today. At least her jeans were dark blue, so if a wet spot was starting to form between her legs it would be difficult to see.

Dominique stopped in front of a display of blindfolds. There seemed to be more different types of blindfolds here than pills in a pharmacy. Dominique looked over the choices and picked one. "This is the Black-Out Blindfold. It's padded, and designed to fit comfortably and tightly over your partner's eyes. A true submissive gets off on not seeing what's going to happen next. It gives you an added measure of control. The sexual tension and anticipation can go off the charts when you use one of these babies."

Veronica looked it over and placed it with her other purchases. They drifted over to an assortment of shackles, handcuffs, and other bindings mounted on the wall. Veronica said, "Wow. There are a lot of choices for all of this stuff. What do you like to use?"

"I have an assortment in the dungeon," said Dominique. She plucked a pair of handcuffs from the wall. "These are a reliable restraint. The guy is not going to escape from them. They are actually the ones many cops use. They double lock and you can secure a man for hours. You can leave your place, go shopping or catch a movie, and he will be there when you get back."

Veronica looked at her friend. "Do you know that from experience?"

"Oh yeah!" exclaimed Dominique. She fingered some heavy-duty straps made from a composite material. "I like these too. They are long enough that you can be very inventive with them. I use these when I'm binding someone to the Pendant. It is only Velcro at the ends but, if you use it correctly, even a strong man can't get out of it."

Veronica stood there for a minute thinking. "I'll go with the handcuffs. I think I need to get used to the basics first." She walked down and stopped in front of a table. She fingered one of the items on it. The construction was wood and it came apart in two sections. One end had a small opening in the center where the two halves met. "Is this one of those Humbler things you told me you used on Xavier?"

"Yes, it is. I have to admit, it is pretty funny the first time a man is put in one of these. Watching them maneuver around is hilarious.

"Sounds very entertaining. However, I think I'll pass on that for now." Veronica shivered. "It does look painful though. What else should I get for my starter kit?"

Dominique chuckled at how Veronica referred to the purchases she was accumulating. "At the least, you should get a crop and paddle. Something that you have to be determined to do is to break your man if necessary. If you remember, Xavier was extremely compliant, but I still had to work on him about cumming without permission. Other guys are going to know what they might like, but they are going to balk when you discipline them...at least in the beginning. You have to make them realize that you aren't going to take any shit from them, or they're going to be left out on the sidewalk, probably trussed up in a Humbler."

"Have you had a sub you had to discipline?" asked Veronica.

"Almost all of them," said Dominique. "And I do mean for real. Not that fake kind of discipline that just adds excitement to the playtime."

"Is it hard to do?"

"It's easier when the man is a true sub. Let me tell you about this other guy I met." Dominique began the story. "It had been awhile since I'd had sex and I was in search of my next slave. I was going though my contacts when I remembered this sexy Spanish guy, Romano, who was a Secret Service agent. We'd met on a sunny, spring day. I was waiting for a pedestrian light to change, when I noticed three men on the opposite of the street. They were all wearing dark suits, the dead give-away badges on their belts and clearly carrying hand guns. They were definitely Secret Service. The light turned and we all began to cross the street. As I walked I couldn't help checking out one of them. He was tall, with a muscular build, and glided towards me with a confident stride. As we crossed we made brief eye contact and, after a few steps, I glanced back over my shoulder only to see that he had stopped in the middle of the street and was looking at me. I continued to the sidewalk and after a few paces realized that he had followed me.

"'Hello', he said with a rich, powerful voice, 'I hope I am not being too forward, but my name is Romano, and I was afraid that if I didn't introduce myself to you now, I may not get another chance.'"

"I was a combination of taken aback and flattered by his straight-forward approach, and my mind was working on the appropriate reply. As you know, a Goddess is not going to give up control, even to guy with a badge and a gun. 'Hello to you as well.'"

"Romano and I looked at each other. He was tall and muscular, with black, wavy hair and dark-brown eyes, and had a subtle, sexy Spanish accent. He went on, 'Look, I really would like to know your name and would enjoy taking you to dinner.'"

"The mild hint of desperation, along with the Spanish accent, tore down the wall I was building and I relented. I smiled and said, 'My apologies, my name is Dominique and yes, I think we can work something out.' We chatted awhile longer and exchanged phone numbers."

"Later that evening, Romano called me and we had a really relaxed, enjoyable conversation. We agreed we would have dinner the next night."

"So Romano picked me up the next evening and we had a lovely dinner together. He drove me back to my place and I invited him up. Once we were inside, though, he started to get a little too frisky. God knows I was hot for him, but he was like an octopus with his hands all over me. I finally hauled off and slapped him as hard as I could. He looked shocked. I saw his muscles tense up, but then he relaxed and almost looked like he was going to cry. He mumbled that he was very sorry."

"What did you do?"

"I read him the riot act. Something you are going to have to learn," said Dominique. "I told him I was the Goddess and his sole desire was to please me. I explained that I was going to make sure he never forgot. With that, I led him into the bedroom. I told him to strip and lay down on his back on the bed. By this point in time, I had installed heavy-duty rings at the corners of my bed. I handcuffed each hand to the upper corners of the bed, and shackled his ankles to the lower corners. He looked delicious, spread eagled like that. He was a little nervous, but his dick was getting hard. He was not as big as Xavier, but he had nothing to be embarrassed about."

Veronica leaned against the table. She could feel the telltale dripping in her pussy again. "What affect did that have on you?"

"I wanted to jump his bones and ride him until I came over and over. However, while we want discipline from our subs, a Goddess also has to learn discipline. I lit the candles I had around my room. Romano's head was swiveling around on his neck like a bobble-headed doll as he tried to follow me. I slowly stripped in front of him. As I seductively pulled down my blue thong, I could see a drop of pre-cum reflecting on the tip of his cock in the candlelight. I could tell he was waiting for me to pounce on him. So, I went into the bathroom instead and took a shower!"

Veronica laughed. "Good move. Let him stew, right?"

"Anticipation is your best friend. I took a long shower. I even played with my pussy a little so that I could have an orgasm to take my edge off. I was in there for a good half hour."

"Did his dick go down while you were gone?"

"It was at about half mast," answered Dominique. "When I stood back in front of him, I reached for my body lotion on the dresser. Again, I took my time as I sensually applied lotion all over my body. When I looked in my mirror, I could see my skin was gleaming in the candlelight. Then I picked up my crop." Dominique went over to a table and picked one up off a table. She handed it to Veronica. "Just like this one. Hang on to it. That will be my gift to you when we get out of here."

Veronica put it with the handcuffs, blindfold, and clothes. She breathlessly asked, "Then what did you do?

"I reached into one of my drawers and pulled out a garter belt and stockings. I gave Romano a good view as I put them on right next to the side of the bed. I could tell by the hunger in his eyes that he wanted me. I put on a real show of attaching the stockings to the straps on the garter belt. I made sure to turn around so that he could clearly see how they circled my ass. When I did this, he moaned. I whirled around and gave his balls a slap with the end of the crop. Romano gulped and I leaned right over into his face. My tits were caressing his chin, but I yelled at him, 'You will only speak when I tell you to. You will never again paw all over me like you did when we came through the door tonight.' I slapped his balls again for emphasis. 'Do we understand each other?' Romano nodded."

"I barked at him again, 'What do you call me?' He looked perplexed and said, 'You are my Mistress.' With that, I hit his thighs, dick, and balls with the crop. If he could've curled up in the fetal position, he would have. I shouted, 'I am your Goddess. Do not ever forget that.' Romano whimpered, 'Yes, yes.'"

"I have to say that this was getting me hotter and hotter. I could also tell it was not having a negative effect on his libido. He was mighty hard and I was getting more excited. I still controlled myself, though. I went over to another dresser. I selected one of my favorite perfumes and gave myself a slight spray on my boobs and right above my pussy. I wanted this to be an assault on all of his senses."

"I realize that he had been hooked up there for almost an hour. It was a good sign that he was not protesting. He seemed to take to the whip pretty good. I went back over to him and seductively dragged the crop over his body. I teased him for a few minutes over his torso and legs, but then concentrated heavily on his balls, cock, and ass. The more I played here, the more he strained against his bonds. He was arching his back so much I thought he would have to see a chiropractor the next day."

"That's the control I want to have over a man," said Veronica.

"And you will," promised Dominique. "At this point, I couldn't stand it any longer. I straddled him, grabbed his cock, and slid the head up and down my soaked slit. When I slowly placed his head about a half of an inch in my pussy, I felt his dick and balls contract. I grabbed them and said, 'You do not cum without permission. That and calling me Goddess are my two biggest rules. Understand?'

"Romano gulped and said, 'Yes.' 'Yes, what?' I yelled as I squeezed his balls hard. 'Yes, Goddess,' he sputtered."

Veronica idly wondered if anyone would notice her grabbing one of the many dildos in the store and retreating back to the fitting room to use it. She knew her panties were soaked. In a whisper she said, "Please go on."

"At this point, I backed off his dick and rubbed my pussy on his leg. A huge wet smear was forming on his thigh and I was slowly jerking him off. He was looking at me wide-eyed and helpless. Without any warning, I leaned forward and took his cock in my mouth. I give him a great show as I took all of him in and then slowly glided my lips back up his shaft. Whenever I felt his balls tighten, I squeezed them and backed off on the sucking. Teaching a man how not to cum takes a little practice.

"When he'd calmed down a little, I got back to sucking his dick. Finally, I decided that humping his leg was not doing anything for me. I stood up, pivoted, and lowered my pussy onto his face. I heard a gurgling sound under me and I told him, 'Make me cum, slave. Now!'"

"Romano was pretty good at this. I could feel his lips and tongue doing what they could in such a position. Since I was facing his dick, I flicked it with the crop and said, 'Faster, slave.' He responded to my orders. It felt really good. Then he did something I didn't expect. He sucked my clit into his mouth and attacked it with his tongue like a boxer hitting the speed bag. He did it so fast that everything I was keeping inside poured out like a violently erupting volcano. You wouldn't have known I'd had an orgasm a little while ago in the shower…so much for keeping the edge off! I may have drowned him under my juices, but he kept going. The suction of his mouth kept my clit tight inside it, and I went through wave after wave of orgasms. I lost count. I finally had to get off him. I turned around and put my nose to his. He was saturated and I could smell my sex all over him. I told him, 'Now, you are going to get fucked!'"

"Romano shouted, 'Yes, Goddess,' almost in relief. 'I am sorry I almost came.' I dropped down on top of his cock. I liked how it filled me. Even after what his mouth did to me, I needed a good fuck. I ground down my pussy and felt his dick go deep inside of me. I just sat like that for a minute, not moving. Then I slowly started to just rock back and forth on him. As I did this, I reached out with the crop and gave his cheek a love tap. 'And no matter what I do,' I told him, 'you will not cum until I tell you to.' Romano just nodded and I could see him concentrating on controlling himself."

Right next to Dominique, Veronica felt like she was coming out of her skin. For a brief second, she imagined herself in the gold body suit with her exposed pussy clamped around a man's steel-like cock. She tried not to moan as she said, "And…"

"I had exercised as much self-control as I could. I went from rocking back and forth to riding his dick as if it was a stallion. I think I kept blurting out 'faster and harder.' I know I started to bring the crop down on his hip like a jockey pushing his horse at the end of the Kentucky Derby. It wasn't long before I felt another wave of orgasm after orgasm. I reached around and felt his balls as I rode. Whenever I felt them tighten, I administered pressure. This seemed to be enough to keep him under control. He never did cum in my pussy. I was proud of how he responded to the discipline. After what felt like my tenth orgasm, I slid off his dick and started to jerk him off. He was so wet with my juices I was able to get a great rhythm going. Then I told him, 'You can cum now, my sexy slave. I want to see the power of your cum. Let yourself go.' Romano lay back in his bonds and relaxed. I could tell that all he now focused on was his cock, and what I was doing with it. I could feel his dick getting even harder and I could actually see his balls constrict. With a yell, he let go a huge spray of cum. No lie, the first spurt hit my ceiling. Then I think he squirted at least fifteen more times until he was spent. He could not move and I draped my body over him."

Veronica bent over at her waist trying to exert some control over her pussy and hormones. Again, Dominique had a gift of making you feel like you were right there watching. She finally got herself under control and asked, "That was it for the night?"

"Hell, no," said Dominique. "After twenty minutes or so, I unchained him. We cleaned up a bit and I started to teach him some other lessons and introduced him to some of my toys. This was way before I lived where I am now. I didn't have a dungeon, but I had a good collection of toys. Other than the Humbler, I didn't start out with much more than you have in your hands now."

"Once again, I feel like I have so much to learn," said Veronica.

"You need to learn at the speed you will be teaching your slave. It is a slow and steady process. If you rush it, you are going to get frustrated."

"Is there anything else I should get now?" asked Veronica.

"I think for your 'beginner's kit' as you so aptly put it, the last thing you should buy today is a paddle." Dominique walked down the aisle and stopped. She selected something that was about the size of a ping-pong paddle, but was made out of wood. It was heavily lacquered and had holes drilled into the surface that went all the way through to the other side. She held it up and said, "This will do."

"What are the holes for?"

"Cuts down on wind resistance. You can get a good whack out of it. It also makes cute patterns on a guy's ass if you hit him there," said Dominique.

"Sounds fun," said Veronica. She took the paddle and her other items to the checkout counter. Dominique took the riding crop from her pile and paid for it as she said she would. Veronica picked up all of her bags and they left the store.

"How about lunch?" asked Dominique, "Shopping always makes me hungry."

"Definitely. Since I had to get to the optometrist so early, I didn't eat breakfast," said Veronica. "Any ideas?

"There's a nice little restaurant right around the corner from here. It's perfect for lunch."

The women strolled to the restaurant, and since it was already two in the afternoon, the place was fairly empty. They were escorted to a table for four. This worked out well for Veronica as she set all of her purchases on one of the empty chairs. They perused the menu and gave their order. As the waitress departed, Veronica said, "I had so much fun today. I'm already looking forward to wearing my clothes and using some of these items for real."

Dominique said, "Like I said, don't hurry it. You should practice using your crop and paddle on one of the pillows on your bed. You want to get used to the feel of everything. There's a fine line between disciplining a man, and hurting him badly. Get a feel for your strength and technique."

"Any other suggestions?" asked Veronica.

"When I get home, I'll text you the names of some really good websites explaining how to be a dominant female. I had the instinct, but I also gleaned a lot from visiting those sites. And don't forget that the Internet also has a lot of shit on it. I do not want you to get hooked up on the wrong sites. If you find any on your own, float it by me first so I can check it out."

Veronica beamed. "Thank you for all of your concern and help. It means a lot to me. I love the outfits we bought today. Do you have time next week to do my makeover? I'm ready to do more shopping!"

"Doing a makeover with you will be fun, Veronica. As I said, you have a great body. It's time for you to put it on display in the correct way. Wearing the right clothes, jewelry, and makeup is a great way to start empowering your self. I saw the light in your eyes when you modeled your outfits. Wait until we do the makeover. You'll be rocking, girl!"

So, next week?" Veronica asked eagerly.

"Actually, darling, we are going to have to wait until the week after next. I have to go to Chicago on Monday for a conference. A group of financial advisors are trying to form an association of supporting women, working in the industry. I want to see Chicago and networking is always a good idea."

"Why network with other financial advisers? Aren't they the competition?"

"In a sense, yes. But I am getting a little frustrated at my company lately. I'm doing so well, the higher-ups should be approaching me for a promotion, but it hasn't been happening. In business, if you don't explore options to advance, you die. I think it's time to let myself get out there a little more. Besides, Chicago might be fun. You never know who you are going to meet." Dominique subtly cupped her breasts and arched her eyebrows when she said this.

"No date this evening?" asked Veronica.

"I'm between guys right now and I feel like I'm in a rut lately. Mentoring you has been a big help. I figure a change of scenery in Chicago for five days wouldn't hurt either."

"We know I'm not seeing anyone right now. What do you think of a girlfriend night at the movies?"

"That's a great idea, Veronica."

Their food came. As they dug in, Dominique and Veronica talked about the movies that were showing and what they wanted to see.

Chapter 11

$\mathcal{D}$ominique sashayed out of the bathroom of her suite enveloped in the big, fluffy robe the hotel provided. She decided that she'd made a great choice by staying in the Four Seasons Hotel in Chicago, rather than the hotel a half a block away that was hosting the three-day conference she was attending. This was her first trip to the Windy City and she was enjoying herself immensely. She sat in the over-stuffed armchair that looked out over Lake Michigan and relaxed. It was a good idea to approach this whole experience as a mini-vacation. It had been too long since she had taken the time to get out of DC. The great thing about this trip is that she could write off the whole thing as a business expense.

She had flown into O'Hare Airport on Monday morning. The conference was running from Tuesday to Thursday, but Dominique was staying until Sunday. She was bookending the business part of the trip with three entire days to do what she wanted. When she checked into the Four

Seasons she was led to the Executive Suite, which she found very impressive. The large window faced the lake and the beautiful spring day bathed the magnificent view in warm sunshine. A small comfortable sitting area was set up in front of the window. Her bathroom felt like a mini-spa and she was looking forward to sleeping in the king-sized bed.

She packed a lot of fun activity into her first day in Chicago. The proximity of the hotel to great shopping made exploring the surrounding area a highlight. After a couple of hours, Dominique returned to the hotel with a couple of beautiful dresses and a new pair of shoes that had caught her eye. She rang down to the hotel's spa and found out they had an opening for a massage and a facial. The masseuse was terrific and worked out knots and stiffness that Dominique had felt creeping into her body for the past couple weeks. As she lay there naked and under the warm draping, Dominique reflected that the massage had been great, but what she could really use was a great bout of sex with a willing man under her control. It had been too long, and sex was a great relaxer. She knew her talks with Veronica got the young woman hot and bothered. The problem was that they had the same effect on Dominique. Like her protégé, Dominique was also taking matters into her own hands for relief.

Feeling wonderful after her massage and facial, Dominique returned to her room and took a nap. She took her time getting dressed after waking. She selected a simple black dress that was comfortable and attractive. What she liked about this dress is that it appeared to just wrap around her, and looked to be in danger of falling down her shoulders and bringing her tits into full view of the world. It never happened, but the danger certainly attracted eyes to her voluptuous figure. She added appropriate heels, makeup, and jewelry to the outfit and went down to the hotel's lounge for a pre-dinner cocktail.

Dominique enjoyed the admiring gazes that followed her path through the lobby and into the lounge. Entering, she got her bearings and went over to one of the small, bar-height tables that were set up off to the side of the bar. Dominique perched herself up on one of the chairs and surveyed the room. It was after six o'clock so there were a fair amount of business types in the place. However, there were also plenty of couples, small groups, and people who looked like they were on vacation. When the waiter came over to take her order, Dominique decided on a champagne cocktail. She felt like something a little different to celebrate being out of DC.

When the drink came, Dominique started to pull out her hotel key card so the waiter could put the charge towards her room. The waiter waved her off. "There is no need for that. The gentleman over there insisted that he pick up the tab for such an elegant woman." He indicated a well-dressed man sitting at the corner of the bar.

"Please tell him I'll let him buy me a drink as long as he joins me with one of his own," said Dominique. She took her glass and saluted her benefactor across the room.

The waiter left and Dominique took a sip. The drink tasted very good. As she set her glass down Dominique started to count to herself, *five, four, three, two, one*. As she got to *one*, the man who bought her drink stood up and picked up his glass from the bar. He started to slowly make his way over to Dominique.

She smiled at the predictability of most men. She also appraised this guy as he walked towards her. He was white, but sported a healthy tan as if he spent a lot of time outdoors. He was at least six feet four inches tall and carried himself with the grace of an athlete. His suit was black with a thin, white pinstripe running throughout the material. His dark hair was cut short and, as he got closer, Dominique could see intelligent hazel eyes peering at her. An easygoing smile gave him an air of friendliness.

He pulled up to Dominique's table and said, "I hope I am not being too forward. I thought you looked like a queen when you strolled in here. I took a chance and wanted to see if you were up for a little company. If you are waiting for someone, or I am interrupting anything, I apologize in advance."

"No, not at all," said Dominique. She indicated to the chair across from her. "Please have a seat. This is my first evening here in Chicago and it would be nice to share a drink. Thank you very much for mine, by the way."

"My pleasure," said the man. "My name is Gordon Walker."

"Dominique La Belle." They shook hands.

Gordon asked, "So what brings you to Chicago? Business or pleasure?"

"Originally business, but I decided to add some time for myself. I am here for a three-day conference that starts tomorrow. How about you?"

"Strictly business. I've developed a new design of golf clubs. I am in town lining up some distributors."

"So you are a golfer?"

"I play strictly as a hobby. By trade, I am an engineer. I have a master degree from MIT. I started playing golf as a kid with my Dad. After college, I was out with some friends and we had a discussion about the equipment we used on the course. When I went home, I really looked at my clubs for the first time. I decided to put some of my engineering skills to work and came up with a design that is attracting a lot of attention in the industry. This is not something that I ever thought I would be doing, but I'm enjoying the challenge."

"Funny how we fall into things sometimes," commented Dominique.

"Isn't that the truth," said Gordon, "What do you do?"

"I manage other people's money. A couple of people who do what I do are attempting to set up a national association devoted to women in my profession. I thought I'd come out and see what it was all about. It starts tomorrow. So I am here with an open mind and determined to have a fun week, if nothing else."

"Where is home for you?" asked Gordon. "I live in Phoenix."

"I'm from the nation's capital, good old Washington DC. From the looks of your tan, it looks like you get outside a lot."

"Lately, I've been out on the golf course a great deal, drumming up interest in my club designs. When I saw you coming through the door it hit me that I've been around men so much lately, that it has been too long since I enjoyed a pleasant conversation with a beautiful woman. So that's why I was attempting to insert myself into your evening."

And what else? Dominique chuckled to herself. "I don't mind," said Dominique. "I love hearing about how someone starts up a new business."

Gordon's smile grew larger. "Wonderful. Do you have plans for dinner? The entire reason I came to this place is that I was meeting a company executive for dinner, but he had a family emergency concerning one of his kids. I found out two minutes before you walked in the room. I am not usually this spontaneous, but there is supposed to be a nice restaurant here and I already have the reservations. It would be my pleasure."

Dominique laughed. "How could I refuse such a wonderful offer? I have no plans and it sounds like fun. Lead on."

Gordon got up and came around to Dominique's chair. He helped ease it back and held out his hand for her to grasp when standing. Side-by-side, they walked out of the lounge area and over to the hotel's restaurant, the Allium. The hostess showed them to a cozy table. They chatted and ordered another drink. As they looked over the menu, Dominique was pleased that the restaurant advocated a farm-to-table philosophy. She liked knowing everything was fresh and that it came from a certified humane farm. They gave their orders and went back to getting to know each other.

Dominique liked Gordon. He was intelligent, handsome, and perfectly comfortable in who he was. Talking was easy and fun. The funny thing was that she did not know if she was sexually attracted to him. She would love to see him naked, but there was something missing that she could not put her finger on. He was not gay, at least not the way he kept looking at her chest. She did not think he was a sub. He did some very benign flirting and seemed to like Dominique. Of course, she knew it was not always love…or lust…at first sight. Dominique decided to keep her options open and see how the evening played out.

She put that thought to the back of her mind and concentrated on having fun. It was a wonderful dinner. The food and service were outstanding and the conversation was great. When it was time for dessert, Dominique and Gordon decided to split a piece of flourless chocolate cake. When that came to the table, along with tea for Dominique and coffee for Gordon, he said, "Look, this may sound like a line, but I really am not someone who goes around picking women up. I had a five-year relationship that ended six months ago and since then, I have thrown myself into my work. But I think you are terrific. Would you like to continue the night? I am staying over at the Ritz Carlton."

"I like you, Gordon, but I'm not sure. I have had a lot of fun tonight. I have to be honest with you, though. I know exactly what I expect from a man in the bedroom and I do not compromise. Things have to be just right for me to be with someone."

Gordon smiled at Dominique's directness. He asked, "And exactly what does 'just right' mean?"

"As I have been detailing to a new girlfriend of mine for the past couple of weeks, I am a naturally dominant woman. I only want a man who will do what I say and follow orders. You said I reminded you of a queen when I walked into the bar. I greatly prefer the title of 'Goddess'!"

Gordon raised his eyebrows. "A dominant Goddess, eh? So I presume you have a dungeon outfitted at home?"

Dominique felt a little anger stirring. She thought he was mocking her. She narrowed her eyes and looked directly into Gordon's. Very evenly, she said, "As a matter of fact, I do."

The handsome man held her gaze for a moment. Then to Dominique's surprise, he burst out laughing. "It figures. You meet someone terrific and then you find out it isn't going to work."

"What do you mean?" asked Dominique. "And what's so funny?"

"You know, I was getting a great vibe that we had a lot in common, but I did not realize how much. I have a dungeon at my house in Phoenix! It's getting dusty from lack of use, but that's how I groove too. I am a male Dom myself. I was going to bring that up before we did anything, but I guess we would just be spending the entire night struggling to see who ended up on top!" He let out a loud laugh again at his joke.

This time Dominique joined in the laughter. "I've been spending these last couple of hours trying to figure out why I didn't feel comfortable taking you back to *my* room and having my way with you. Now I get it. My instinct was correct. It was just very vague."

Gordon leaned back in his chair with a big smile. "This is the first time this has ever happened. I have never tried to get to know a woman before who was a female counterpart of what I am."

Dominique explored her memory for a moment. "Same here. So was the woman you were with for five years your sub?"

"Yes. We were in love, but then something happened. The love part got stale or started to fade away. The sex was still great and she never stopped serving me, but we thought it was best for both of us to part ways. With getting my new business off the ground, I haven't thought about being with anyone. Then you came through that door and I had this vision of you in my dungeon. I have this chain on a pulley that I handcuff a woman to and then pull her arms above her head. I thought of you naked in that position and I was sitting at the bar getting hard. Unfortunately, there must have been interference in the air, because I guess the only vision I should have had of you in a dungeon is you running it!"

"If it helps," said Dominique, "I wondered what you would look like strapped naked to a device I have at my place." She sighed. "I have to work on that. I can pick up on a subservient man, but I have to start reading the ones who are dominant. I have met many who thought they were Doms, but they were just pretenders. They were actually easy to break."

"I run into the same thing with women. Tell you what. Let's head back to the bar for a nightcap. We can at least compare notes."

As Dominique sat at the window on Tuesday morning after her shower, she smiled at the thought of the rest of the evening she'd spent with Gordon. They'd talked so long about their experiences that they closed the bar down. They exchanged stories and ideas. They each had pictures of their playroom on their phone and shared those images with each other. Dominique told Gordon how she was starting to take Veronica under her wing, and he shared how he mentored a school friend in dominant disciplines a few years ago. Gordon's girlfriend had enjoyed being a subject that the new Dom could practice on under Gordon's supervision.

As the night came to a close, they had hugged in the hotel lobby. They exchanged business cards and Gordon said he would contact Dominique the following week when she was back in Washington. During their talk, he had confided that he had a few million dollars of cash coming in from the new business and he needed help with what to do with his money. Dominique reflected that not only did she have a nice time and made a new friend, but it looked like she had a new client as well. She had a good feeling about Gordon and thought he was going to do very well in business. There was nothing like taking on a new client, especially just as they were poised to grow quickly.

Dominique got out of the chair and removed her robe. She went over to the window and looked out. If anyone was looking in her window, she hoped they were enjoying the show. While she and Gordon were not a match, her pussy had been hot for cock ever since. Their conversation had the same effect on her as talking with Veronica. Hopefully, the next handsome man she connected with would be more of what she craved.

She started to pull her clothes out for the first day of the conference. The first day would probably be boring. She had her doubts about a group of financial advisors forming their own association, but she was open-minded.

When she showed up, she figured there were about 70 people there. The majority were from the Midwest and Dominique was happy to see that a fourth of the attendees were women. She chatted with many of the participants and most were friendly and open. It was nice to interact with people from outside of the DC cut throat lifestyle for a change. Three women who were from different financial houses in Chicago invited Dominique out to dinner with them. She took them up on the offer and the chance to make new friends.

The four of them found out they had something in common with their situation at work. By any standard, all four women were high achievers at their firms, but they did not receive the same promotions as their male counterparts. As one woman said, "It's just another good reason to have a dick!" Dominique joined in the laughter, but she realized these women needed to empower themselves in their jobs. If they gave the impression of being doormats, they would never get the promotions they deserved, no matter how well they performed. She did not say anything that evening, but wondered if she would have a chance to bring this subject up at the conference.

This matter occupied Dominique's thoughts as she chose her wardrobe for dinner. She decided to wear one of the dresses she bought here in Chicago on Monday. She had left it for the hotel to press and it looked great hanging in the closet. It was bright red with a tiny strip of black outlining certain aspects of her figure. When she put it on, Dominique liked how it highlighted and drew subtle attention to her tits. It was also just short enough to show off her calves and thighs, but still appropriate as business attire. She really thought she should do a seminar for women on dressing for success. Whoever decided that it was only appropriate for businesswomen to wear black or navy blue pantsuits or jacket/skirt outfits should be drawn and quartered. It was probably a man! Dominique smiled as she thought of devices she had at home that would adequately torture the culprit.

She fastened on the matching shoes she'd bought when she found the dress. They were an intricate combination of straps and bindings that attached three-inch heels to her feet. She finished getting ready and walked the short distance to the hotel where the conference was being held. This was also a nice place, but it did not have the pizzazz and elegance of the Four Seasons.

Going through the lobby, Dominique made her way to the main ballroom. Entering, she noticed the room was a bit more crowded than the day before. She mentally took note of the new arrivals. Dominique kept an extensive file system of people in her head – it was one of her strengths in business. She could easily remember people she had just met, along with any pertinent information about them. This proved invaluable in many ways. When she was debating whether to attend this event, she'd decided that at the very least she would utilize it for its networking potential, if nothing else.

The day proceeded with various sessions meant to showcase the reasoning behind forming a new association of financial planners. Dominique felt ambivalent on the merits of the entire enterprise, but she enjoyed the interaction with people and contributed her opinion to some of the discussions. She met the new faces in attendance and found out that most of them were top senior management from various firms. Based on the questions some of them asked her, Dominique realized they were using this gathering as an opportunity to troll for new talent for themselves. She decided that this must be what a professional football player felt like when he started to test the free agent market. For all its problems, Dominique liked her firm in DC and had rarely thought about moving somewhere else.

The day drew to a close, and there was one session left. Then there was to be a cocktail party at the hotel for all participants. The following day's session only went to noon, and Dominique expected this second day to actually be the last day for many of the attendees. The discussion at this session centered on how the formation of an association would help members negotiate the road to promotions. Near the end of the scheduled time Dominique saw Anne, one of the women she had dinner with the previous evening, raise her hand, "Do you think something like this would help promote the women professionals?"

The leader at the podium was a short, tubby man in his fifties who had not changed his hairstyle since 1983. He was one of the masterminds behind this event. He looked at the woman over his glasses and said, "I am sure that if a woman shows the same dedication and success as a man, this will be helpful to her in moving up the ladder."

Anne pressed him. "Well, that doesn't happen now. I don't see how it will change anything."

The man looked at his watch. "That is about all the time we have for today. All I can say to your statement is that if women worked as hard as men in this business, they wouldn't have a problem. I will see everyone at the cocktail hour."

You could almost hear all the women in the room suck in a breath at once. Dominique saw red and leaped up and met up with the man, as he was about to exit the ballroom. She cut across his path and stopped right in front of him before he could leave. He tried to slide around her but Dominique nimbly kept in front of him. He looked up at her and said, "May I get by?"

"Sure. In a minute," Dominique answered. "But first you have to tell me if you really believe what you just said up there about women."

"You mean about working as hard as a man and then they'll get ahead? Yeah, I believe that."

"Do you work with any women?"

"We have a couple of administrative assistants in the office…"

"Assistants!" Dominique exploded. She started to maneuver him over to a corner so they would not be blocking everyone else leaving. "You mean you have no women on your level?"

"Nah, I'm in a small office in Indiana. People there wouldn't want to deal with a female anyway."

Dominique lowered her voice. "Listen, you pathetic excuse for a man. If you are going to get up to talk to a group, please do not be so apparent about your ignorance that everyone in the room sees it. Do you know what a woman has to do in this business to succeed? We have to out-work and out-think every man on our staff, so that our numbers are so far ahead the bosses cannot get rid of us. Then you know how we are thanked? We aren't. We get to keep bringing in the big bucks, but when a promotion is open, it goes to another member of the 'good-old-boys' club."

"I really think you are overreacting, and I have to go." The man made to push past Dominique who stuck her hip out to block him.

"You idiot. I am the only one keeping you from getting beaten up by the other women in this group. You want to start an organization that helps the profession and you are too much of a dope to even know what is going on!! Maybe you need to head back to Indiana tonight. Perhaps do a little research on the Internet and see how things are still so unequal between men and women in the workplace, especially this industry. If you have trouble with the big words, I am sure you can find someone in your farm fields to read it to you."

"How dare you," the man sputtered.

"Believe me, friend, you do not want to dare me on anything. I have taken on men who are bigger, smarter, and tougher than you and had them calling out for their mommies. And they loved every minute of it." Dominique paused to catch her breath and then suddenly backed away. "Get out of my face. I just realized it isn't hard to find men who are bigger, smarter, and tougher than you. I just have to find a middle school around here."

The color of the man's face almost matched the shade of Dominique's dress. It looked like he didn't know whether to yell, cry, or let his head explode. He did the smart thing and scurried away.

Dominique composed herself and turned around. To her amazement, about half the room was still there watching her. They broke out into applause – the men and the women. Dominique smiled at them and went back to her seat to gather up her belongings. A few people came up to her and congratulated her on educating the speaker. A couple of men escorted her down the hall to the cocktail event. They both commented that they could see what was going on in their offices, where their bosses did not treat women as equals, and it was a shame. They were still too low on the totem pole to do anything about it, but they wanted to make changes whenever they got into a position of power.

Entering the room where the cocktail reception was being held, Dominique could see that her opponent was nowhere to be seen. As she headed to the bar for a glass of wine, she thought to herself that he must have had some brains. If he'd come to the reception, the other women would have held a tag team match and gone after the poor slob a lot harder than Dominique did!

As she took a glass of wine from the bartender, Dominique turned around and saw a man in his forties approaching her. She remembered his name as Charles and knew he was one of the people who had shown up today. He worked for one of the large firms right here in the city, but she did not remember his title. He put out his hand, "Charles Simmons. That was impressive back there."

Dominique shook it. "Dominique La Belle. I am not in the habit of doing that, especially in public. I was just shocked at his ignorance. Not only did he not know what he was talking about, he didn't care that he didn't know. I felt like somebody had to speak up for the women in the room."

"I thought you handled it very well. I especially liked how you steered him away from everyone. I don't think anyone heard exactly what you said to him, but the body language was fun to watch. It was as if you were stepping on an insect, but kept your poise as a lady." Charles took a drink. "And a very beautiful lady at that."

Dominique sized up the man. He was about six feet tall, trim, and had a graceful air about him. He was dressed in chocolate slacks, with a tan sport coat, and a white shirt open at the neck. His eyes were a deep brown and his dark hair had a touch of grey around the edges.

"Well, aren't you full of compliments? So, you don't agree with that jerk's assessment of women?"

"I'll let you be the judge of that. I have five Vice Presidents reporting to me at my firm. Three are women, one is a brilliant young man from England, and the fifth is my brother. All of the women are there on their own merit. Unlike the gossip you hear around this city, I did not sleep with any of them, they earned their positions. I promoted the English chap because he is damn good at his job, and I like the continental touch of his accent. My brother is a VP because, well, he is my brother." He rolled his eyes. "I did promise Mom I'd look out for him."

Dominique gave a chuckle. "Well, I am impressed, both for promoting women and for listening to your mother. My company is not so progressive."

"I believe you mentioned somewhere today you are from Washington?"

"That's right. And I have to say that I have been enjoying your city. It's the first time I have been here. I even helped add to the economy. I picked up this dress and these shoes on my first day here."

Charles looked down at Dominique's shoes. She could see his eyes widen and a small sheen of sweat sprout on his forehead. "My God, they are beautiful. And such lovely feet." He looked back up at Dominique with wide eyes. "I didn't think of this in the other room, but I can visualize you dancing on that idiot's back with these beautiful, flaming red heels." Then he added in a quieter voice, "Do you like to do that with men?"

If this were a game show on television, the lights and sirens would be going off all around Dominique. He was a sub, and one with a foot fetish at that! This realization triggered a warm feeling deep in her pussy. "You have no idea," she purred.

Charles took a gulp and finished his drink. He looked at the empty glass. "I need a refill. Let me get you one. I think we should grab one of those tables and get a plate of those delicious smelling appetizers. Let's talk for a bit about how work differs between Chicago and Washington."

They did just that. The talk was mainly business. Dominique found out that he started his own firm at thirty, after working at a major financial company for eight years. He built it up over the next fifteen years until it became the largest independent firm in the Windy City. Dominique also found out that he lived about an hour outside the city. He was divorced with two teenagers who preferred living with Dad rather than their mother.

Dominique liked this man on many levels. Finally, she asked, "So tell me, Charles, how long have you liked shoes on women?"

"It's not the shoes, Dominique, but the woman they are attached to. I think you are exquisite. I have a good sense of who you are, so I will tell you this. I am the head of a multi-billion dollar firm. I enjoy being the face of my company and I love bringing in new business and making money. But behind closed doors, I ache for someone I can serve. I have been like that ever since high school. I need the woman to be in charge. The reason I got divorced is that I gave my wife everything, and that is the one thing I wanted from her. And she couldn't do it. There were a couple of half-hearted tries, but she did not have it in her. It has been a long time since I met a woman with even the potential to know what she was doing in the bedroom."

His little confession started to soak Dominique's panties. She thought, "The hell with it. I am in a new city. This is a nice guy who is powerful and kind of hot. I want some fun tonight." She looked directly in his eyes and said, "Charles, I am a half a block away at the Four Seasons. Want to escort me back to my room?"

Simmons looked like he'd just won the lottery. "It would be my pleasure, Dominique. Tell me, how do you prefer being addressed?"

Dominique leaned over and whispered into his ear, "I am your Goddess."

They stood up and casually left the room together. They easily went back to talking about work. Before either of them realized it, they were exiting the elevator at the Four Seasons and stopping in front of Dominique's door. She opened it with her card. They entered the hotel suite and Dominique sweetly said, "Why don't you wait here, while I go into the bedroom and prepare things for us?" The smile on Charles' face grew from ear to ear as he thought his wildest dreams were about to come true. Dominique gently stroked his cheek in almost a concerned way, as if she was trying to calm a frightened pet. Charles shivered at her touch and was left wondering why he suddenly felt a little trepidation.

After five minutes of waiting, Dominique finally told him to strip and then come into the bedroom. Charles gleefully ripped off his clothes off and hurried in. Entering the room, he came to a sudden stop as he saw Dominique completely naked in all her glory – her long black hair cascading across her shoulders, her huge brown breasts jutting out like oversized melons, her large bubble butt sticking up and ready for action, her toned arms and legs, and (he gasped) her beautifully manicured feet! Her toenails were painted candy-apple red.

Dominique's figure was awe-inspiring. She was ultra-curvy in all the right places and yet was fit in all the other places. Most women who are curvy are not that fit and most women who are fit are not that curvy. Dominique had achieved the unique status of being a perfect combination of both. It was as if her body knew where to channel her calorie consumption to maximize her sexual attributes. She had the measurements of a female comic super-hero come to life.

Charles began panting audibly, like a dog, and Dominique once again appreciated her effect on these poor men who sought out her attention. Dominique laughed, "Calm down, boy. We haven't even started yet."

Charles regained control of him self and replied, "Sorry, I've just never seen anybody like you before."

Dominique's voice took on a serious tone and said, "It's not often a mortal gets to meet a Goddess."

Charles nodded in agreement and asked, "Well, since we are both naked, should we begin?"

Dominique laughed uproariously at Charles' naive question. "WE aren't doing anything. However, YOU can begin performing for my pleasure."

Charles didn't know how to take that and asked, "Well, what do you want me to do?"

Dominique pointed to the bed where there were two sets of lingerie spread out. "Which one do you think will look hotter, the pink camisole with the crotch-less pink panties or the dark purple bustier with the frilly purple thong panties and black stockings?"

Charles didn't want Dominique's feet to be hidden behind the stockings, so he said, "The pink one would look sexier on you, I think." Charles was already dreaming about what her body would look like in it with her perfect feet exposed!

Dominique said, "Great choice, now you put them on."

Charles' mouth dropped open and Dominique laughed at this foolish man's situation. Did he really think she was going to dress up for him and spend the evening pleasuring him? She smiled. He was here for her satisfaction and needs. Like all men, he had to learn the hard way that he would find his pleasure in serving her.

"You mean, like, put them on the way a girl would?"

Dominique laughed again, "I know it looks complicated, but don't worry, I'll help you with all the straps and clips." Dominique helped dress Charles as if he was a teenage girl, and by the time she was done with him, he looked like one! "Now go look at yourself in the mirror and tell me what you see."

Charles shuffled nervously towards the bedroom mirror and gasped, "Oh my...." He stood there in shock at the sight of himself pretty in pink. He felt like a little, helpless puppet to this woman he had just met. He would have laughed if any other woman had tried to dress him up like a girl but, for some reason he couldn't quite understand, he felt the need to do whatever Dominique commanded. It was almost as if he had taken on the role of being Dominique's daughter and she was his stern mother. Dominique loved the process of emasculation and Charles' transformation had only just begun.

"Well," said Dominique, "Don't you look like a little darling?"

Charles felt ashamed at doing what this woman wanted just to play with her feet. However, Dominique had the most beautiful feet he had ever seen, and he was willing to do anything to touch them. And now it appeared that Dominique really was going to make him do anything and everything to earn that right! He would just have to play along and eventually he would get his reward.

"You know what? Charles is too manly a name for you. You look more like a Chelsea dressed up like that. What do you think, Chelsea?"

Charles responded, "Yes, I like that name, it sort of sounds like Charles."

"Who?" mocked Dominique, "I don't know anyone by that name. All I see is a little pink-panty-wearing slut named Chelsea who will do anything to play with my feet, right Chelsea?"

"Yesssssss," Charles eagerly replied.

"'Yes' what, Chelsea? Remember, I am your Goddess."

"Yes...Goddess" said Charles at last.

"I see, we need to go over a few things, Chelsea."

Charles winced when Dominique spoke, as every time she made a point to call him by his sissy name, Chelsea, to drive the point home. It was as if she was stealing his identity and programming a new one for him. This woman was dangerous!

What surprised Charles the most was how excited he was getting at this role reversal game. His cock began to twitch and rise up out of his crotch-less panties.

Dominique noticed this too and arched an eyebrow. "Well, you are indeed a little slut, aren't you Chelsea? What is that sticking out of your panties?"

"My cock, Goddess,"

"Not anymore, Chelsea. That looks to me like a big clit. Why don't you rub your clit for me?"

Charles immediately grabbed his cock and started furiously jerking it up and down. At last thought Charles, I get to have a boner and jerk my cock in front of this gorgeous woman. That was another fetish of his.

However, Dominique crushed this dream as well and said, "Stop! That is not how a little girl rubs her clit, Chelsea. She doesn't jerk it up and down like boys. She rubs it gently back and forth. Now, let me see you rub your clit." She paused, "Chelsea."

Again, that damn name, thought Charles.

Charles began slowly rubbing his cock while Dominique continued to amuse herself by teaching him how to flick it lightly with his fingertip and rub it gently in circles to hit the right spot. Since he had an uncut cock, Charles had to pull back the foreskin to rub it.

Even then, Dominique mocked him, "Pull back that clitoris hood and expose your clit to me. Tell me what you are doing, as you do it. I want to see if you are following my instructions on clitoral arousal, Chelsea."

"I am pulling back my foreskin, I mean hood and rubbing my cock...I mean clit."

"Good girl," applauded Dominique, "you took to becoming my little slut very quickly a little too quickly, actually. Most men resist and fight back, but not you. It's almost as if this is naturally who you really are. A naughty little girl wearing pink panties and rubbing her clit, right Chelsea?"

Charles was also shocked at how quickly his manhood had become subsumed in his new sissy persona. Why did he give in so easily to this woman? What power did she have over him so suddenly that no other did?

Dominique lay back on the bed and she said, "Well, I am not interested in watching you pleasure yourself no matter how ridiculous you look, Chelsea. Put yourself to use and start massaging me, from my head down to my toes." At this, Dominique wiggled her toes, which drove Charles mad with desire for those feet. But first, he would have to work his way down this woman's beautiful body to get to the prize!

Charles sat to one side of Dominique and began rubbing her neck in smooth circular motions. Dominique relaxed and gave herself over to Charles' touch. *The man, oops, girl definitely knows what she's doing,* laughed Dominique to herself. Charles went down her back and worked out every knot and kink. Dominique's bodacious ass was begging to be handled, and he asked, "Goddess, may I caress your butt?"

"Certainly Chelsea," replied Dominique, "please do."

Charles slapped a lot of oil on his hands, as he had a lot to work with, and kneaded Dominique's puffy ass cheeks back and forth and up and down until he had a good rhythm going. He looked down her legs and saw her feet that so badly needed to be massaged by his expert hands. He started to slide his oiled up fingers down Dominique's legs, but she turned around and said, "Now the front, Chelsea. I can orgasm from having my breasts fondled in just the right way, so I want to see how good you are."

Charles sighed to himself and poured a large amount of oil on Dominique's huge breasts. Just like her ass, there was more than ample to work with there. He cupped them, squeezed them together, rubbed them outwards and inwards, but it wasn't until he touched Dominique's rock hard nipples that she let out a moan. Sensing her pleasure, he began stretching her nipples out and rubbing them between his fingers. Dominique clutched Charles' head and forced his mouth down on her nipples saying, "Suck them Chelsea, suck your Goddess's breasts."

Charles pushed her huge breasts together until the nipples were practically touching, then he proceeded to suck on both nips at the same time, doubling Dominique's pleasure. After sucking for a few minutes with Dominique writhing underneath him on the bed, Charles tried to break the seal and get some air. Dominique grabbed his head and held his mouth on her nipples, forcing him to continue sucking. Charles' face was smothered in Dominique's boob flesh and he didn't know how much longer he could suck before he passed out. Dominique's breathing got faster and heavier as she neared orgasm and would not let go of Chelsea's head until she had got what she wanted from her little princess.

Finally, Dominique came hard and felt her pussy throb as that delicious feeling washed over her. A tit orgasm was completely different than a pussy or clit orgasm and she loved it because it was rare. She lifted Chelsea's head off her nipples and watched as she gasped for air. Charles gulped in all the air he could after his marathon suck session and finally opened his eyes and saw the Goddess smiling below him. Dominique said, "You ok? Good, now you can continue the massage down my legs."

Charles rubbed Dominique's quads and hamstrings and could feel the muscle tone rippling underneath her soft skin. It was amazing how this woman appeared to be hard and curvy but was really soft and curvy once you felt her. Her body was almost to sexy, but yet every man's dream.

As Charles went down to her calves, he began salivating at the thought of touching Dominique's feet. He was so close now, everything had been worth it: the shame, the indignities, the wait and at last, her feet would be his to caress and that would make him rock hard and blow his load. His hands slid down her ankles and just as Charles closed his eyes in ecstasy, Dominique pulled her legs up in a ball and out of Charles' hands.

Charles let out a cry of despair and Dominique laughed. She said, "Do you really think you deserve to touch your Goddess's feet? Ask yourself what have you done to deserve that ultimate pleasure?"

"B-b-but,' Charles stammered, "I did all these things for you, I thought I would be rewarded?"

Dominique shook her head. "You still don't understand, Chelsea. You did these things for you. You exist to serve me and when I feel like I want my feet to be caressed, I will tell you to massage them. My pleasure is your pleasure. When you understand this concept, then you will be worthy of touching your Goddess's feet, if I so desire."

Dominique noted the look of bemusement on Charles' face. He was not a true sub. He acted like one and professed to be one, but when it came down to it, he really only wanted his pleasure, not Dominique's. She would have to let him go, as he was not worthy of her and probably never would be. She sighed. It was too bad though, as he really did have great hands and knew how to use them! However, Dominique never lowered her standards, not even for momentary pleasure. The search for her true submissive would continue.

Chapter 12

*I*t was a week since Dominique had returned from Chicago. It was a beautiful, warm day as she took a seat at an outdoor café. It was 9:30 in the morning and she was waiting for Veronica. The two of them agreed to meet for brunch before setting out on some shopping. This would actually be the first chance they'd had to chat since Dominique's return. One thing about taking a week away from the office is that Dominique had been overloaded with work for the past week. Her two assistants had done a great job while she was gone, but they could only do so much. This was the first time since being in the Windy City that Dominique seemed to have a day for herself.

The waiter brought her orange juice and tea. As she sipped the juice, Dominique saw a cab pull to the curb a half a block away. Veronica stepped out and made her way to the café. She was simply dressed in black jeans, sandals, and a cream-colored, sleeveless blouse. She had pulled her dark hair back in a ponytail this morning, and Dominique noticed she did not have glasses on. The new contacts must have arrived. It made a huge difference without having the glasses hiding Veronica's pretty face.

She leaned down and hugged Dominique, "It is so good to see you back. I am sorry you were so busy this week that we barely had a chance to talk on the phone. Are you all caught up at work yet?"

"Just about. I have to admit it was a long week. When I fell into bed last night, I found myself looking forward to today. It is a relief not to have to go to the office."

The waiter came back over and Veronica ordered coffee. Then the two women picked up the menus and decided what they wanted for breakfast. They gave their order when the waiter returned with the coffee. Then they caught each other up on what they had been doing in work all week. Finally, Veronica said, "You told me on the phone about a guy you met in Chicago. Have details to share?"

Dominique laughed. "Looking to get horny from my encounters?"

"It's better than nothing…which is exactly what I've been getting around here. Yes, I want to hear about him."

"Well, there were actually three of them. I met this one man on my first night there. We had a lot of fun at dinner and all. He wanted to take me to bed, except we found out we were both dominant. Since a clash of wills does not make for a fun time, we decided to just be friends. He may become a client for me though."

"Was he cute?" asked Veronica.

"More than cute. We both wanted to know what each other looked like naked, but it was not going to happen. My last day there I met an ambassador. I'll tell you about him later. He was fun and his business takes him to DC quite a bit, so I may see him again soon. The one I wanted to tell you about this morning is named Charles and it will be a good lesson in how to totally dominate a man in mind, body and soul. Charles visited the conference I was at on Wednesday. He owns one of the larger independent financial firms in Chicago and he was there to see what talent he could find for his company."

Veronica smiled, "Oh, I think I am going to like this one."

Dominique proceeded to tell her the story of how she emasculated and denied "Chelsea" her fun for not properly worshipping Dominique as her Goddess.

When Dominique finished, Veronica had beads of sweat showing on her forehead. She looked flush and was breathing hard. She reached out, took a glass of water, and downed a big gulp. "I guess you had a good time in Chicago," she said with a shaky voice.

Laughing, Dominique said, "Yes, I did. I can't speak for 'Chelsea' however," and both women laughed.

Their breakfast order came and the women dug in. Veronica tried to concentrate on the delicious food, and not the wet feeling she had down near her pussy. She understood what Dominique meant about a Goddess needing the discipline to not give in to her own momentary pleasures when she had a lifetime to acquire her pleasure the right way. Veronica knew she wanted the same thing, but she was determined to do it on her terms for a change.

Veronica said, "I want to do what you do with men. I'm ready to try it. I'm not sure how I will do though."

"As I said once before, it will be easier to do the more experience you get. From where I sit though, you are missing one important thing."

"What's that?" asked Veronica eagerly.

"A man," said Dominique laughing.

Veronica joined in and let out a large laugh. "That's something I wanted to talk to you about. I did meet someone last week while you were away."

"Oh, do tell."

"There's a coffee shop near my apartment. I ran into this hot guy there. He was having trouble finding the right kind of milk for his coffee. You know how they have all of those selections in those places. Anyway, I helped him out and we started talking. He'd just got a job working with one of the lobbyist outfits in town. He is very nice and seems very sweet. I'm not sure, but I think he might like having a woman tell him what to do."

"What makes you think that?" asked Dominique.

"It was in the way he talked with me. Like I said, he is very hot, but does not act that way. You know how guys who are attractive seem to know it, and then act like assholes? He was not like that at all. It was just in his demeanor and the way he talked."

"So you liked him?"

"Definitely. I am not sure what he thinks of me though. I did let him know that I was no wallflower. I just reached into my inner Goddess and it seemed to work. It felt very natural once I tapped into that. I don't know if I have the "hotness" factor in me though. We do have tentative plans to go on a date next Friday night."

Dominique sat back in her chair. She finished her tea as she quietly appraised her friend. She was pretty and could be downright beautiful with a little work. She knew from what she saw at the sex store a couple weeks ago that she had a banging body. Except, she could not very well show up on a date in one of those outfits. Maybe she could wear one later in the evening, but not to start things off!

She said to Veronica, "I think it's time to have our next shopping day. It's still early. Are you ready for a total makeover?"

Veronica looked steadily into Dominique's eyes. "Yes, I am. I need to start making this happen for me. I trust you with whatever you want to do. I know you have style and all I want to do is learn from you."

Dominique pulled out her cell phone and made a quick call. She spoke for a few moments and looked up at Veronica with a smile. "We're starting out well. The woman who does my hair had a cancellation. We'll start there. With a little hustle, I think you'll be amazed with what you look like in about eight hours from now." With that, the women paid their bill and Veronica followed Dominique's lead. They found a taxi and Dominique gave the address to Salon Cece.

Getting out of the cab, Veronica saw that it was only a small place and she followed Dominique inside. As she entered the salon, Dominique announced, "Hello, ladies. This is my friend Veronica." The receptionist greeted both of them and asked if they preferred red or white wine. "Red," said Dominique as she continued, "I want you to pretend that Veronica is Cinderella. Tonight is the big ball, and I need you to make her the sexiest Cinderella ever. She is already pretty, as you can see, but you have to make her drop dead gorgeous. Let's do the works with her hair and manicure and pedicure. You don't have all day. I still have to get this gal some clothes and make-up."

Chandita the stylist who did Dominique's hair, descended on Veronica. The young woman felt a little embarrassed being the center of attention, but she let Chandita take charge. The hairdresser whisked her over to the sinks where a shampoo girl washed Veronica's hair. When that was done, Chandita placed Veronica in a chair in front of a mirror. She slowly circled Veronica and tried to get a feeling for what would look fantastic on the girl. Veronica had high cheekbones and a long neck. She should be able to do something to accent those features.

Veronica watched Chandita moving around her. "Do I get to look at some pictures or something to choose a hairstyle?"

Her stylist emphatically shook her head. "No. Leave this to me."

Dominique who was watching from a nearby chair sang out, "Trust her, Veronica. She knows what will work best on you."

Veronica took a deep breath and relaxed. "Ok. Go for it," she said.

Five more minutes went by as Chandita continued to study her subject. Then there was a flurry of scissors, brushes, and blow dryers for the next hour. Veronica felt the woman cutting, teasing, and pulling her hair all over. The only thing she knew for certain was that her ponytail was now gone. Chandita had spun the chair around so that Veronica could not watch the progress in the mirror, but she could look through the hair falling in front of her eyes and see Dominique nodding in approval at the work being done.

Finally, her stylist slowly turned the chair around so that Veronica could see herself in the mirror. She sucked in her breath. The woman that stared back at her looked beautiful. Her hair was shortened and pulled back into a pile on top of her head. Two little curls came down on either side of her face. The effect was pleasing. Turning her head to the side, Veronica could see how it gave a different look to her neck. The word "elegant" leaped to mind. She actually reminded herself of old movies she had seen with Audrey Hepburn. Looking forward again, she thought that her look was different in this view. With the curls falling down, it gave a playful look to the style. Veronica thought, *Playful and elegant, I can live with that.* Aloud, she said to Chandita, "You are amazing. I never would have thought of this for me."

The woman thanked her with a big smile. "The nice thing about this haircut, it is very easy to get back into this style. It will fall very nicely when you want to be casual, and you can get it like this with about five minutes work. Hair should be beautiful and practical, not time consuming."

Dominique was now standing by the chair. "I love it. It is helping me crystalize some wardrobe choices for you. Now go over to that table there and get your nails done. Your hands look like you build houses for a living."

Veronica followed her instructions and another woman went to work on her hands. Dominique came over and helped choose a neutral color for her nails. She told Veronica that the first order of business was getting her nails looking good again. Once she got in the habit of that, then she could play with color choices and even match a color to a specific wardrobe selection when desired.

When her nails were complete, Veronica went over to have her feet and toes worked on. The same girl who worked on her fingers massaged, scraped and soaked Veronica's feet. When she was done, she finished off by using the same nail polish on the toes that she'd painted on the fingernails. When everything was finished and dried, Veronica and Dominique got ready to leave. Veronica paid her bill, tipped everyone generously, and thanked them profusely. She had never felt so pampered. Every time she caught a look at herself in the mirror, it took Veronica a second to realize she was looking at herself. The new look would take a little getting used to.

Going outside, Dominique and Veronica hailed another cab. Dominique told the driver to take them to the Tysons Corner Mall. Turning to Veronica, she said, "I'm going to take you to a couple of stores I used to go to all the time. I found many great outfits there and they almost always have great sales. The truth is that when you are starting out, you have to be a Goddess on a budget. Xavier got me into some clothes and shoes that I was working my way up to buying, but his generosity jump-started some of my wardrobe choices. Hopefully, you'll meet a man like that but for now, you'll do pretty well at the places we're going."

"Thanks for being so considerate. I appreciate all you have done, it means a lot to me. "

"No problem," said Dominique. "If I can get another woman to realize the power that she has in her, then I did a great job. Besides, you can buy me a drink later." She smiled.

"At the least," said Veronica.

It was not long before they got to the mall. Once inside, Dominique took the young woman's arm. "The first thing we are going to do is show off those beautiful tits of yours. I saw them when you were trying the outfits on at the sex store. Most of the time you seem to downplay them with what you wear. Is that what you do?"

"Uh, no. I never really gave it much thought."

"Well, you need some new bras. Do you realize that most women wear the wrong size bra? We are going over to a shop that specializes in bra fittings."

Dominique lead her to a store called Rigby & Peller. Inside, Dominique went up to a sales lady that she obviously knew. She instructed that her friend be properly fitted with comfortable, sexy bras. They should also lift and display her assets as much as possible. The sales lady smiled knowingly and took Veronica into the back. The clerk came out several times, chose some bras, and went back to Veronica. Finally, both of them came out with Veronica holding four different bras.

Veronica was smiling and said, "Geez, I never felt so comfortable in a bra before. I have to say that I like how I love how they make me look."

"Good for you," said Dominique. "Now I have two pieces of advice for you. Get a pair of matching panties for each bra. Personally, I would go thong, but that is up to you. Then go back into the changing room and put a set on to wear out of here. You might as well have on one of your new bras when we try on some dresses and tops."

Veronica picked out four matching thongs and then took the black bra and thong with her to the dressing room. She came out a couple of minutes later. Even with the blouse she was wearing, Dominique could see that her breasts were lifted and looked much bigger. She knew this was only because her bra was now doing a better job of pushing up her tits. Dominique nodded. The girl's upgrade was progressing nicely.

Their next series of stops were several shops that had stylish clothes at a reasonable price. After getting an idea of the cost, Veronica said that she would be comfortable getting at least four different outfits today. She looked at Dominique, "What do you think I should get?"

"I'm thinking we will go for three outfits suitable for dating or just going out on the town. We are going to go for sexy and powerful. We will do the same for the fourth outfit, but we will tone the sexy back just a hair. I think it is important that you buy one outfit for work that will knock your boss and everyone else on their ass. Remember, we are grooming you for a lifestyle change, not just where dating and men are concerned. Once you have these, then you can slowly add to your wardrobe as time goes on."

With those parameters in mind, the women started to explore the stores. Veronica tried on many different outfits. In the beginning, Dominique thought her choices were too conservative. With her coaching, Veronica started to branch out and try on outfits that were shorter, tighter, and more revealing. Dominique watched the transformation as Veronica began to see her potential as a hottie.

The afternoon wore on as the women lost count of the number of outfits Veronica tried on. When she finally decided on the four she was going to buy, Dominique nodded her head in approval. As the girl paid for her purchases, Dominique went onto her phone again.

As Veronica came back with her bags, Dominique said, "I think we need to take you out for a test drive. Let's go back to my place. You can shower there if you want and we can go out for dinner and drinks. Maybe we can go dancing. But I want the new Veronica to get all dressed up. I just called a friend of mine, Rose. She does make-up for the major theatres here in town. I've asked if she would come over in a couple of hours to work on you and give you some make-up tips. How does that sound?"

"Sounds amazing. I have to say this entire day has been a little overwhelming. I want to get dressed up in one of these things." She held up her bags. "But I will only do it on one condition."

Frowning, Dominique asked, "What's that?"

"That dinner and drinks are all on me tonight. All of this has me feeling terrific and I want to thank you."

"Then you have a deal," said Dominique. "Let's see if Washington DC can handle two hot women tonight!"

As they were heading back to her place with all of Veronica's purchases, Dominique texted her friend, the make-up specialist. By the time Veronica came out of the shower, Rose had arrived with her case of goodies. She was a tall, thin woman with upswept, dark-brown hair and dressed all in black. When Veronica came into the living room wearing one of her new bra and panties, Rose gave her an appraising look.

"You were right, Dominique, she is a cutie. It is much more fun to add to beauty instead of trying to manufacture it for someone average looking." To Veronica she asked, "How experienced are you with make-up, sweetie?"

"I use the basics," Veronica said shyly. "My Mom showed me when I was younger and I had a professional do my face when I went to my prom, but that is about it."

"Well, we are going to use the make-up table and mirror in Dominique's room. I will explain what I am doing and I want you to pay close attention. That will help you later when you are doing this to yourself. You have a very pretty face, so it is not like you'll have to spend hours in front of the mirror."

"I know you can do good things with her," said Dominique. "I'm glad you were free."

"I'm in between shows for a week, so this was great timing."

The three women went into the bedroom. Dominique perched on a chair and watched Rose work on Veronica. Rose carefully told the girl what she was doing and why. She gave suggestions about what colors and types of cosmetics would work best with Veronica's eyes and complexion. Rose worked with a subtle hand as she made Veronica's face look even more alive and vibrant. Dominique saw that the girl was enjoying the transformation to her looks. She smiled when Rose's hand accidentally dropped to Veronica's breast and the young woman gave an involuntary shiver.

When she was done, Rose turned Veronica around and with a sweeping hand gesture said, "Voila!"

Dominique grinned widely at the result. Veronica's eyes seemed to glow and she'd gone from pretty to beautiful. Dominique marveled at her friend's skill. She really was an artist! She had not been heavy-handed at all with applying make-up and the result was exquisite. Dominique clapped her hands, "You look great, girl. Now go figure out which one of your outfits you want to wear."

When Dominique and Rose were alone in the room, Dominique asked, "Do you want to go out with us tonight?"

"Thanks, I'd love to but my Mom is in town. I'm taking her out for some fun. So Veronica is the gal you told me about the other week?"

"Yes, I am her Goddess mentor. I have to say, I have been enjoying the whole thing. It is a kick helping a woman find herself. It is a process, though. We have been doing this bit by bit. Soon she'll be ready to fly out of the nest on her own."

Rose laughed, "Hey, don't forget it's also fun to fly with others." Her eyes twinkled.

"You still hang out with that swinging crowd over in Maryland?"

"Yup. They get together for different house parties twice a month. I do try to get to at least one of them. There is just something about an orgy that relaxes me!"

It was Dominique's turn to laugh, "Maybe that's where you should take your Mom."

"Hey, don't laugh. I'm scared that if I suggested it, she'd take me up on it. She is only 53, has a hot bod, and has more of a dating life than I do. With some of the stories she tells me, I think she could get into it. But I have my limits. I don't think I could play with people if my mother was watching."

"That'd be way up there on the kinky scale," said Dominique. The two embraced at the door. "Have fun tonight with your Mom."

"You too. Don't hurt them too bad, I know how you dress. I think you and Veronica will make quite a pair tonight. Enjoy!"

With that, Rose left. As Dominique softly closed the door, she thought about what she was going to wear. She mentally went over the contents of her closet. She decided to wait and see how Veronica dressed. After all, Dominique did not want to wear something where they clashed.

She went into her kitchen and pulled a bottle of Kendall Jackson chardonnay out of the refrigerator. She poured two glasses and went back into the living room. She sat one down in front of the sofa as she leaned back in her favorite chair and sipped. She was having a good time with Veronica and Dominique felt like the girl was really getting a lot out of their friendship. She saw flashes of a Goddess in the young woman and she hoped she could teach Veronica how to make it shine like a blazing sun.

As she sat there waiting for Veronica to emerge from the bedroom, Dominique began to wonder how many other women were out there who needed help to bring their true selves to the surface.

Dominique had an innate sense of people. It was one reason she was so good in helping her financial clients. Many times, she seemed to know how a client wanted to invest their money before he or she did. She also realized that she was that way with her girlfriends over the years. She understood who they were or what they needed to make them blossom prior to any real in-depth conversation she may have had with them.

It did not stop with women either. She had a talent for recognizing what men wanted and she was very good at pushing their buttons. With some, it was raw physical sex when they were together because they were in that type of relationship. For others, like her boss Marcus, it never went past a certain boundary. She could control the situation within established parameters, or at least *her* boundaries, though there had been more than once when she knew Marcus was ready to pole vault over the fences she set up. Still, other men who were only platonic friends came to her for advice on the sexual aspect of their relationships. She had given suggestions and advice to them that fired up their sex lives with their respective partners.

Dominique took another drink and sighed. All of those people out there who needed help that she could provide. Ideas started flying around in her mind. They were not in any concrete form yet, but she could feel a tug at her consciousness where she knew there was a calling to her life here. How she would respond to it was vague, but she was confident that if she let the concept stew for a while, she could bring it all together.

Her reverie was broken by the appearance of a beautiful young woman coming into the room. Veronica had dressed in a bandage, sapphire-blue dress that seemed to fit her like a glove. The deep scoop in front filled with her pushed-up breasts to the point that she looked like she grew a cup size in the past five hours. She paraded back and forth in front of Dominique like a runway model. The heels she had on accented her strong calves and the dress were short enough to showcase her muscular thighs. As Veronica walked across the room, the dress happily hugged her shapely ass. Dominique was not sure, but it seemed as if Veronica had amped up the wiggle in her ass. Whether on purpose or the effect of turning into a "new woman," the effect was quite exquisite.

Dominique clapped her hands, "That's what I am talking about, girl! What do you think?"

Veronica stopped with a hand on her hip and one leg out to the side. "I have to say, I almost didn't recognize myself in your mirror. This sounds bad, but I wish my sister was here so she could eat her heart out."

Dominique laughed aloud as she stood up. "That's the attitude we want. Now, have a seat there. I poured you a glass of wine. Feel free to put on the TV. Now that you are finished, I need to go get ready so that folks will see two Goddesses out there partying tonight."

She went into her bedroom and jumped in the shower. Drying off, she contemplated her wardrobe and decided that a cream dress would complement Veronica's blue. She had a new dress she had purchased in Chicago but had yet to wear out for an evening. Putting on a red bra and thong, she sat at her table and expertly applied her make-up. She then slipped the dress over her head. Studying the effect in the mirror, Dominique nodded in approval. It did highlight her curves nicely! She adjusted the front so that ample cleavage showed without her bra peeking through. After that, she went to her jewelry box and chose a couple of rings and bracelets to accent the outfit. The final touch was a pair of slinky red shoes that did everything for her legs that Veronica's shoes did for hers.

Dominique came back into the living room where Veronica was finishing her wine. She put the glass down and stood to look at Dominique. "You look HOT," she blurted out.

"WE look hot," Dominique, corrected her. "Now before we go out and one breath of wind messes up these beautiful female forms, let's take a picture together." She went over to her purse and pulled out her smartphone. "I am not one for selfies, but we look too good not to take a picture!"

Laughing and giggling the two women stood next to each other as

Dominique took several photos. For good measure, Veronica got out her phone and did the same. They both looked at the results on their screens. Dominique said, "I made a good choice in this dress. I think my cream makes your blue pop and vice-versa."

"I know," squealed Veronica, "and I am still having trouble recognizing myself. I think we are going to have a good time tonight!"

"I do too. So where do you want to go for dinner? I am famished."

"Me too. It isn't everyday a girl gets a total makeover. I took care of reservations while you were getting ready. I meant what I said before. This evening is on me."

With that, Dominique and Veronica set out on the town. Veronica had made reservations at the Capital Grille in DC. Dominique was used to having every man, and most of the women, follow her with their eyes when she came into a room. For Veronica, it was new, and something she was going to have to get used to happening. As luck would have it, their table was at the other end of the restaurant. As they followed the maître d through the maze of tables, most of the patrons took in the sight of the two beautiful women. More than one guy was chastised by their dinner partner for gazing at the two goddesses for too long!

Dinner was excellent as the two enjoyed salads, steak, and even split a dessert. They laughed a lot and did not care who knew they were having fun. Veronica told Dominique that she loved dancing, but it had been a few months since she really got out and moved, so once they left the steakhouse Dominique took over the itinerary for the night.

They ventured out to several different clubs over the course of the evening. Wherever they went, men flocked to them. They certainly did not have to buy a drink for the rest of the evening. Both women danced with a variety of partners, all of whom they wore out on the dance floor.

Though they had not talked about it, Dominique and Veronica seemed to know this was a night for fun, and not necessarily to pick up any men or be picked up by any man. Dominique watched as Veronica grew in confidence as the evening wore on. A few short hours ago, she almost seemed to be like a girl who was playing dress up when she stood in the living room. But now, she seemed to be the sexy, vibrant woman that she wanted to be. The dress was no longer a costume, but became a real part of her. She seemed to instinctively know how to walk and carry herself in the outfit, but everything really seemed to come together when she started dancing. All her parts moved in a seductive manner that had men drooling around her. Veronica took all of this in stride as she danced, talked, and flirted.

Dominique had more than her share of admirers to keep busy, but she often looked over to make sure her protégé was okay. The one area where Dominique knew Veronica needed a lot of coaching was to be selective in the man she wanted to be with. Most of these guys here would fuck her at the drop of a hat, but would not take to being dominated. That came with time and practice. As for herself, Dominique didn't find anyone there that enticed her, so she was content in her own dancing and flirting.

Somewhere around 3:30 in the morning, the women returned to Dominique's townhouse. Standing in the middle of the living room, Dominique pointed out the guest bedroom where the girl could crash for the rest of the night. They were both light-headed and feeling good.

Before heading to her room, Veronica hugged Dominique and gushed, "Thank you so much for everything. I've never felt this good before. It was like I could've had any guy there eating out of my hand if I wanted."

"Just remember to use this power for good and not evil. Now get to bed and I pray to the Goddess that you are not an early riser. I am beat."

The women broke from their embrace and went to their respective beds. Veronica fell asleep thinking about all of the men who'd flocked around her. Dominique drifted off thinking that there was something here that she could share with other women…and men too. Her last thought was that she knew she would figure out how to do it.

Chapter 13

*I*t was the following Friday and Dominique sat at one of the little tables off to the side of the bar at their favorite place. It had been a long week at work. Her clients loved her but she was starting to feel very unappreciated by the men who ran the company. Marcus was a vocal advocate for her to the powers-that be, but once again she had been passed over for a promotion to partner. It had gone to a guy who did his job well enough, but Dominique did not think he could match the profit that she brought to the firm. She was never one to give in to the TGIF philosophy, but this was one week that she was glad was over.

At around three, when Dominique had been sitting at her desk, she took a quick call from Veronica. The girl asked if they could meet for drinks after work. Dominique thought she sounded a little stressed and said she could meet at around seven.

Dominique finished her business day a little bit early and decided to head over to Four Courts in Arlington to enjoy a drink by herself, before she met her protégé. Sitting there and nursing her wine, she smiled as she remembered the fun she'd had last Saturday. Between the shopping during the day and the partying at night, Sunday had been a day of chilling out and doing a whole lot of nothing. Veronica had left at a little after noon. She was still euphoric about the night before and talked a little about how she was going to reveal her new self to that nice guy she had met at the coffee shop.

Dominique froze for a moment with her glass halfway to her mouth. It dawned on her that when she and Veronica had last talked on Wednesday, the girl was definitely going out on Friday with that man. Being it was now seven on Friday; it did not seem to bode well for Veronica.

As she was pondering this, Dominique saw Veronica come into the bar area. She was dressed like she used to be and had on a simple white blouse, jeans, and carelessly flowing hair. When she saw Dominique, Veronica rushed over to the table. She clambered up in the chair across from Dominique and simply said, "Hi. Thanks for coming out to meet."

Before Dominique could respond, the waiter came over and asked Veronica what she wanted. She thought for a minute and said, "I need something stronger than wine. How about a gin and tonic? Heavy on the gin, please."

The waiter shuffled off to the bar and Dominique appraised the young girl. Last Saturday she'd seemed so vibrant and alive, and tonight she looked shriveled up and small. After a few seconds of silence, Dominique raised an eyebrow and said, "I'm a little concerned about you. Should I be?"

The waiter came back over and set the drink in front of Veronica. She took a long pull from it, looked up at Dominique with moist eyes, and said, "Remember I told you I had a date tonight with the new guy?"

"Yup."

"Well, Wednesday night he called me up. His company was sending him out of town and he had to leave today. He said he was free on Thursday night and if I was, he would love to get together then instead of waiting."

"That's good."

"I was really happy. It's been so long since I've been on a real date and this guy, his name is Brian, seemed to have it all together. But then it all went wrong." Veronica sniffled and reached for her glass again.

"Tell me about it," Dominique said softly.

"He wanted to do the normal, first date thing. You know, go out to dinner, talk, and get to know each other. I dressed to the max. I liked how people reacted to my upgraded appearance at work and I was feeling good about myself. I dressed up in the clingy emerald green dress I bought on our shopping spree. I got my hair and make-up looking as good as it did on Saturday. I thought I looked terrific and was even ready ten minutes early. My roommates were blown away and loved my new look. I had butterflies when he knocked on my door."

"What was Brian's reaction when he saw you?" asked Dominique.

"His jaw dropped. For a few seconds he was speechless. Then he said, "Wow!"

"That seems like a heartfelt compliment."

"It was. As we walked out to his car, he did say he was a little overwhelmed with how beautiful I looked. I think it was the first time in my dating life that I felt invincible."

"So how did the rest of the date go?"

"Great. We went to a fabulous restaurant and had a wonderful time. We laughed and talked and flirted back and forth. It was as if we had known each other for months. I really got the impression he needed a woman to take the lead in any type of relationship. When we were walking back to his car, he tentatively took my arm, turned me toward him, and kissed me on the cheek. I looked in his eyes and decided it was time to go with my instincts. I took his face in my hands and kissed him as passionately as I felt at that moment. He responded quickly and kissed back just as hard. I could feel my new thong starting to get soaked and I could feel his erection pushing into me."

"When we broke, he had a big smile on his face. I told him that if he had time, we could go back to my place for a while. Both of my roomies were at a night class at Georgetown and wouldn't be back till eleven or so. He looked cute and excited all at the same time. He almost tripped over himself as we went to his car."

Dominique asked, "So you decided you wanted to have sex with him?"

"Definitely. He did too, but if I hadn't suggested it, nothing would have happened that night."

"Tell me more about him."

"He is just what I like. He is tall, a little over six feet. He is very fit with brown hair that is a little long and beautiful hazel eyes. Even though I could see he was trying to downplay his erection, I had a feeling he had a nice package from what it looked like through his pants and what I could feel poking me."

"This all sounds great, but I know it doesn't end well. Keep going."

"Not ending well is an understatement," said Veronica. She drank more of her gin and tonic and continued. "We got back to my place and it was delightfully empty. We have all had people over at different times, but I was happy to have the place to myself for Brian's first time with me. Especially since I wanted this to go the way I wanted it."

Dominique smiled at the fire that lit up the girl's eyes for a second. "Go on."

"I took him into my bedroom and we started kissing. I thought it was important to show him who was the boss right from the beginning, so I stopped with the kissing and backed away. Brian was actually panting, but then again, so was I. When I felt my desk chair behind me, I turned it around and sat down. I looked at Brian and as coolly as I could, I told him to undress. He just looked at me for a moment. I got a little more forceful and said, 'Now!' He smiled a little and started to unbutton his shirt. His chest and arms were very muscular and just a little hairy, which was exactly how I like my men. He looked at me and blushed a little as he started to unbuckle his pants. I am almost positive that he'd never had a woman do this to him before. He seemed to really be getting into it and liking it."

"So he didn't object to any of it?" asked Dominique.

"Not at all. He took off his pants and socks and was standing there in those boxer-brief things that hid nothing. His dick had to be sticking straight out seven inches and straining the material. Finally, he hooked his thumbs into the waistband and pulled his underwear off. My room is small and when his cock sprang out, it would have hit me in the face if I'd leaned forward a little. I wanted to jump on him right then and there."

"But you didn't?"

"Not at all. You would have been proud of me. He shaves his cock and balls and I could see the tip of him dripping. It was sheer willpower for me not to taste him right then and there. Instead, I motioned with my hand for him to turn around. He did and I thought he had a perfect butt. Actually, I thought he was of those few guys that look great absolutely naked. As he stood with his back to me, I took my riding crop and gently dragged it up his leg until it touched his ass. I made a little motion for him to spread his legs and then I tapped his balls with it. Brian pushed the crop away and said, 'Whoa, what do you think you're doing with that thing? Not with the family jewels please.' I said, 'What's wrong baby, can't you take a little pain with your pleasure?' I was getting totally turned on."

"So am I, listening to this," said Dominique. "So far, you seem to be doing well."

"I thought so. I stood up and reached around him. My left hand grabbed his cock and I used my right arm to pull him back against me. I lightly bit into his shoulder. He gave a little yelp and I felt his dick throb. I thought he was going to cum then. He fought it off and turned around. His hands came up and he grabbed my tits through my dress. This was a little too frisky. God knows I was hot for him, but he was like an octopus with his hands all over me. I finally hauled off and slapped him as hard as I could. He looked shocked. I saw his muscles tense up, and his fist roll into a ball. But then he relaxed and said almost philosophically, 'Wow, that's the first time a woman has ever hit me.' I said, 'You'll have more like that coming if you don't do as you are told.' He laughed and said, 'Oh? I'm actually a boxer at my college and could easily block them. Then what will you do?'"

"Well," said Dominique, "What did you do?"

Veronica said, "I read him the riot act. Something you are going to have to learn, I told him, is that I am a Goddess and your sole desire should be to please me. I explained that I was going to make sure he never forgot this lesson. With that, I pushed him down on his back on the bed. He didn't protest at all until I used some scarves to tie each of his hands to the upper corners of the bed, and his ankles to the lower corners. He said, 'you know, foreplay usually begins with me licking your pussy and you sucking my cock. Why are we wasting time?' I got angry at his dismissive attitude to what I was trying to achieve. 'We wouldn't be wasting any time, if you behaved and did as you were told.' He looked delicious, spread-eagled like that, and since his cock began to get really hard, I assumed he was loving his new subservient position."

Dominique leaned forward, "What effect did that have on you?"

"I felt like it was time for me to take control and I was ready to do just that. I strolled walked over to my dresser and picked up my cellphone and started my sexy playlist. Then I slowly placed scented candles on the headboard of my bed. As I reached over top of Brian to light up the candles, my breasts gently brushed against his face. He tried to lick my nipples and I quickly moved away from him. My pussy was so wet and I wanted him so badly. It took everything in me not to jump on him. I went into the bathroom to calm down a bit and to fix up my hair. I left him tied up and alone for a few minutes."

Dominique laughed, "Was his dick still hard?"

"No, because he had actually untied his wrists and was leaning back on one of his elbows jerking off his cock! He clearly wasn't taking me seriously as a Goddess and thought this was going to all be about sex and his pleasure. I said, 'If you want to have sex tonight, you have to be restrained first. No touching me or yourself until I decide.' Brian groaned, but took a long look at my body and said, 'Oh all right, I'll play along. Tie me back up.' He paused and laughed and said, "Goddess."

"I tied him back up and turned my back on him.

"I saw the candle burning and thought up a great idea from a video I had seen once. I picked up my riding crop in one hand and a candle in the other. I held the candle over him. He arched his eyebrows and asked, 'Are you a Goddess or a witch?' To punish his insolence, I poured some of the hot wax from his knee to his upper thigh. He yelled, "Yo, what the fuck?" and yanked his restraints really hard. I said, 'You have to be punished, with either fire or leather,' indicating my riding crop.

"I whirled around and gave his balls a slap with the end of the crop. Brian looked at me in shock and surprise. A look I had been waiting for all night, so I slapped his balls again and said, 'do we understand each other?' Brian responded, 'If you keep slapping my balls you are going to kill my hard-on. Do you understand that?'

"I yelled at him again, 'What do you call me?' He looked perplexed and said, 'Oh right, Goddess.' With that, I hit his thighs with the crop and was about to smack his dick, when he caught the crop in mid-swing and took it from me. I shouted, 'I am your Goddess! Do not ever forget that!' Brian shook his head, 'Please Veronica, enough of the games. I like you and think you're hot, so why can't we just bring this to its logical conclusion and start fucking?'

"I knew I was losing control of the situation and could see that he was topping from the bottom. However, he was mighty hard, which got me more excited," I have to say, I am somewhat impressed with how you are handling his resistance," said Dominique.

"I was too, at that point," said Veronica. "And it felt so natural to me. I then told him the rules you instilled in my head. 'You do not cum without permission and that acknowledging me as a Goddess at all times are my two biggest rules. Understand?' Brian gulped and said, 'Yes.' 'Yes, what?' I yelled as I squeezed his balls hard. 'Yes, Goddess,' he sputtered."

Dominique was wondering where this all went wrong. So far, Veronica had performed well for a first-timer.

"I figured this would help teach a man how not to cum."

"You got that right," said Dominique.

"Then I said, 'You've learned to obey like a good slave and now you will get rewarded.' Brian shouted, 'At last, let's do it!' I agreed, but only if I could have it my way. Brian liked the sound of that and, after I tightened his bonds a little more to make sure he was helpless again, I dropped down on top of his cock. I liked how it filled me up; I guess I just needed a good fuck. I ground down my pussy and felt his dick go deep inside of me. I just sat like that for a minute, not moving. Then I slowly started to just rock back and forth on him. As I did this, I reached out with the crop and gave his cheek a love tap. 'And no matter what I do,' I told him, 'you will not cum until I tell you to.' Brian just nodded and I could see him concentrating on controlling himself.

"By then I'd exercised as much self-control as I could. I went from rocking back and forth to bouncing up and down on his dick, liking riding bareback on a wild horse. I think I kept blurting out 'faster and harder.' I know I started to bring the crop down on his hip, pushing my stud horse across the finish line. It wasn't long before I felt wave after wave of orgasms, but I didn't stop. I reached around and grabbed his balls as I rode, squeezing them whenever I felt them tighten. This seemed to be enough to keep him under control and stopped him from cumming in my pussy. I was really pleased with how he responded to the discipline."

"I'm having trouble seeing what went wrong," said Dominique.

"I'm getting to that part now. After all of those orgasms, I felt one more huge one building up. When that one happened, it felt like my entire existence was centered in my pussy. My whole body spasm for what seemed like hours. I don't know what it felt like to Brian inside of me, but he suddenly shouted, 'Get off. Now.' I was so lost in my orgasm that I just slid off to the side of him. Suddenly, his dick erupted and out came spasm after spasm of hot cum, which sprayed everywhere and landed all over my bed and me. I was covered in it."

"After what you put the guy through, I'm not surprised," said Dominique. "How did you deal with him after he came?"

"I thought about disciplining him for coming without permission, but I never got the chance. With the force of his orgasm, his hands came out of my scarves. Brian sat up and proceeded to get dressed! When I asked him what he thought he was doing, Brian said, 'Veronica, that was some great sex. But I don't know if we're compatible. I think it might be best if we just leave it at a night of great sex and go our separate ways.' I was flabbergasted. I said he looked like he was really enjoying himself. He told me it was hot in the beginning, but he had never been ordered what to do by a woman before. It was not the reaction I expected. I just sat there and started to cry. Some Goddess, huh?"

Dominique realized she had let her little bird fly out of the nest without enough flight training. Her mind raced to figure out how to fix this. Her brain continued working as she said, "So how did the night end?"

"I continued to cry. When I looked up at him he wasn't looking at me, but I could tell he felt really awkward. After a few minutes, he just left and never said goodbye or anything. I don't think I'll hear from him again."

Veronica drained her glass and signaled for another one. She sat there dejected and looked up at Dominique. "What did I do wrong?"

Dominique thought for a moment and said, "Two things come to mind. You may have read Brian wrong. He may not have been as submissive, or desired it, as much as you thought. The other thing is that maybe he is still trying to find himself. He may have the nature of a sub, but has no experience. You took a guy who'd never taken "Being a Slave 101" all the way to a graduate course."

"I thought with the stories you told me of some of the men in your life, that any sub would be wired for this," stated Veronica.

"No, and that is my fault. I haven't told you about the men whom I had to teach how to be a good sub. If I'd come on gangbusters like you did, they would have run away too."

Now tears were trickling down Veronica's face. "I totally messed up."

"Everybody is different," said Dominique. "If you didn't already know it, some men get really weird after they cum. They orgasm and they lose interest in everything you are doing. If that happens, they are more interested in just having playtime instead of a desire to be your slave. With Brian, however, I think you just came on too strong."

"He seemed to like what I was doing at first."

"To a certain extent, he did," said Dominique. "After all, he had a hot woman taking control of him and the sex. But there can be too much of a good thing, especially in the beginning."

"So I have to learn to dominate in stages."

Dominique nodded, "Partly that, but as a Goddess you have to understand how the person you are with is feeling. Have you ever been dominated in a relationship?"

"I have had guys make me feel like shit."

"That's different. That's just the man being an asshole. What I mean is, have you ever had anyone do to you some of the things we have been discussing since we met?"

Veronica thought hard for a minute. She slowly shook her head. "No, not like those."

Dominique stood up. "Finish your drink. We are heading back to my place."

"What are we going to do?" asked Veronica.

"Don't ask me anymore questions," barked Dominique. "Are you a Goddess?"

"Well, after last night…"

Dominique got up into Veronica's face, "Do you have a Goddess inside of you?"

Veronica stuttered, "Y-Yes."

"Then I don't want to hear another word from you until we get to my house. Got it?"

"Yes."

"Yes, what?" If it was possible to shout when whispering, Dominique had just pulled it off.

Veronica's eyes widened as she realized what was expected. "Yes,

Goddess."

"Good. Now go get us a cab. I'll be right out."

Veronica turned and scurried out of the bar. Dominique smiled as she beckoned the waiter over to pay the bill. This was going to be different, even for her. However, she realized that there was something important she hadn't considered in mentoring Veronica. The girl had the makings of a naturally dominant woman. Dominique could see that. However, she did not fully understand what that meant. To bring this home to her, Dominique was going to have to show Veronica what domination actually felt like.

Chapter 14

*T*hey rode to Dominique's in silence. Dominique impassively looked out the window but she could see in her peripheral vision how Veronica kept shooting glances at her. She knew that the young woman was nervous, but that was okay. Inside, Dominique sighed and thought to herself, *I guess this is what you would call tough love.*

The more she thought about it, the more Dominique figured this was the correct approach to take. Everybody was different. Growing up, Dominique had always been comfortable bossing around boys and letting them know she was in charge. For someone like Veronica, she had the need to dominate men, but did not fully understand what that meant.

When they entered her home, Dominique guided the young woman right to the dungeon. As she turned the soft lighting on, she told Veronica to sit in the chair near the Pendant. When she sat down, Dominique walked over and leaned on the Pendant. She said to Veronica, "You know it took me a long time to get this room like it is. If you remember, when I was with Xavier, I improvised with things I found to dominant him as a slave. Then I went out and bought a few toys and over the past seven years or so, it grew into this. We all have to crawl before we walk. I forgot to confirm that in all of our talks. I had you going at a gallop, instead of starting with baby steps. I've certainly learned from that experience."

Veronica was watching Dominique with rapt attention. She realized the Goddess had come right from work to the bar and was still wearing the burgundy dress and black stilettos that she had been in all day. While Veronica was disappointed in how things had ended with Brian the night before, the thing that really made her sad is that she felt like she had let Dominique down. After all this woman had done for her, she wanted to be a student that impressed the teacher. She started to say, "No, you did great…"

"I'm doing the talking now," stated Dominique firmly. She noted with satisfaction that Veronica sunk back into the chair. "Now, as I was trying to say, not all of my men were success stories. I told you about Romano? Well, even though I saw him again, I learned with experience that if a man wouldn't respond properly, no matter how hot I thought he was, I should get rid of him and forget about him faster than a politician forgets a promise. What you have to learn is the difference between a real sub and a pretender. You also have to be able to judge when you need to bring someone along slowly. Understand?"

"Yes," Veronica said quietly.

"Yes, what?" said Dominique.

"Yes…Goddess?" Veronica said louder.

"That's better," said Dominique. Her hands caressed the intricate metalwork of the Pendant. "I have had a lot of fun with this. It is the centerpiece of the Dungeon. It allows me to bind someone in whatever position I desire, so that I can do whatever I want with him… or her."

Veronica felt a chill go down her spine. She felt herself start to get wet as she stared at Dominique in awe.

Dominique liked that look, but she was used to seeing it from her male slaves who were stunned into submission by her whips, slaps, and verbal humiliation. Dominique had learned how to be dominant by simply jumping in and doing it. Sometimes immersion was the best way of learning a particular skill. The girl had done okay with Brian up to a point. Her failure had been in not gauging her man's level of submission. Every man can be dominated, just not by every woman.

Dominique went over to Veronica and slid her hand softly behind the young girl's neck. Veronica purred up against it as if she was being petted. Suddenly, Dominique squeezed hard the way a mother cat would on her kitten's neck, to achieve total control and obedience. It worked. Veronica tensed up and then went limp in submission.

Dominique said, "Kiss my lips."

Veronica had been waiting for that offer since the first day she had met Dominique. Her Goddess had naturally thick, moist lips with an especially pronounced Cupid's bow. She stood up to kiss Dominique on her sensual mouth. Dominique's hand was still cupped behind her neck, while the other went to Veronica's waist for total control as she drew Veronica in slowly. First, their big breasts touched and Veronica felt a tingle shoot through her body. Then when their lips came together, Veronica got suddenly wet and she gave herself over to the sensation of another woman's lips on hers. But this wasn't just another woman! This was a true Goddess and Veronica responded to that power dynamic.

It had been a while since Dominique had dominated another woman and she liked how it required a softer touch than when she was punishing her male slaves. Her males reacted to pain as an addict would to drugs. First, a little pain got them going, then as they built their tolerance level, they needed more and more pain to be controlled. Dominique was more than willing to escalate their pain thresholds, as the less she held back the more empowered she became. She loved the slaves who could take her at full force, where she could lash and strike as hard and as much as she wanted without recourse. This always released her endorphins and got her naturally high. She never used hard drugs; she just used her slaves hard.

But Veronica was going to be different, and as their lips touched, Dominique began licking the outside edge of Veronica's lips, tracing the vermillion curve all around and getting them moist with anticipation. Veronica's mouth was open and Dominique slipped her tongue inside, now caressing the inside of the young girl's mouth as she had done the outside. Veronica's legs buckled slightly before she caught herself and began circling her tongue against Dominique's. Dominique pulled out and flicked her tongue under Veronica's chin, which sent shivers through Veronica's body. Then with Dominique's hand still cupped behind her head, Dominique guided Veronica over to "The Cross."

Veronica opened her eyes and saw where this was leading. She instinctively pulled back and out of Dominique's grip. Veronica then saw the look of disappointment on Dominique's face and she instantly walked to the cross to regain her favor.

"Why did you pull away? Come here," Dominique, admonished her as she pointed to the cross. "This is your problem. You can't hesitate. Your slave will sense any lack of confidence in you and you will lose control. So it's very important not to think, but to act."

Dominique then commanded Veronica to undress, which Veronica did without any hesitation.

At once, Dominique swiftly handcuffed her hands and ankles to the cross. The Goddess reached over and grabbed a pair of Japanese clover nipple clamps from the shelf. Dominique loved having these clamps in her arsenal. Made from two clamps joined by a chain that hung between them, when the clamps were placed on nipples, they tightened every time the chain was pulled.

Dominique took the clamps and placed them on the tips of Veronica's nipples. When the clamps closed, Veronica let out a cry. Dominique laughed and shook her head, "No, no, no! Tell me how good it feels. I only want to hear sounds of pleasure coming out of your mouth. Now, not another cry from you. The more it sounds like you are hurting, the more hurt I will punish you with. Pain begets pain." With that said, Dominique pulled the chain ever so slightly to tighten the clamps on Veronica's nipples a little more.

Dominique appreciated the girl's discipline as she took the slowly increasing pressure without a sound. She was definitely willing to learn. "Look down at your tits," Dominique commanded. Veronica just realized she had been looking at Dominique the whole time and only now looked down. She saw a big pair of gorgeous breasts with large, fully engorged nipples sensually pinched by high-class steel clamps. Then she realized these were *her* breasts! She had never imagined they could be so sexy, so prominent, so dominating! Even though her tits were being handle by another woman, she vicariously felt their potency and knew she could make any man do what she wanted with these two weapons of desire. Dominique saw the look of joy on Veronica's face and knew she was seeing and feeling what Dominique felt. Veronica had learned the power of her breasts.

Once this teaching point had been made, Dominique took Veronica down from the cross. She knew it was time to escalate the sensations of pain and pleasure. Dominique guided Veronica over to a unique device that she had specially designed for her needs. It consisted of a bench shaped like a camel's back, with the hump wrapped in soft fur that rose on an incline, with four posts at the corners. As Veronica turned towards Dominique with a quizzical look on her face, Dominique squeezed Veronica's right tit and said, "There will be no hesitation when I tell you something from now on, got it?"

"Yes, Goddess," Veronica gasped.

Dominique looked down. "Your nipples are STILL hard. I'm beginning to think you like this. Stretch your arms out like you are on The Cross and hold the posts the same way. This device is called "The Hump." Lay on the bench and do not move."

Veronica looked amazing with her ass propped up over the hump and her breasts jutting out to the right and left of the narrow inclined rest. Her feet were touching the posts by the end of the bench and her hands were gripping the posts at the front. Meanwhile her chin sat on a curved headrest that enabled her to move her head up and down like a bobble. Veronica did as she was told and Dominique went over to a cabinet. Out of Veronica's view, Dominique quietly removed her dress, bra and panties, leaving only her thigh-high stockings and high heels. She then turned her attention back to the cabinet and rummaged inside. She pulled out a flogger, dildo, handcuffs and a black bag, and placed them on a nearby table. Then she reached up, grabbed something, and returned to Veronica.

Dominique began talking, almost to herself, ruminating out loud on her philosophy of domination. "It should be exciting but also enjoyable for both Goddess and slave. It's a give and receive relationship. If the Goddess is in tune with her slave, she will know when the slave is ready to fully submit, body and soul." Dominique slipped her finger in Veronica's pussy to see what affect all this was having on the girl. It was soaking wet as she slid her finger in deeper. Veronica pushed back and let out a moan and a gush of cum went all over Dominique's hand. Surprised, but happy to find out that Veronica also was a squitter, Dominique said, "Mmmmmm, now that's a wet pussy. I'll take that as a sign you're ready to be trained."

Veronica gasped out a "Yes, Goddess," and did as she was told.

Dominique grabbed her right hand and fastened it to one of the posts with a Velcro strap. Then the same thing was done to her left. Dominique went to her feet and hitched them up to the posts at the bottom of the bench. When Dominique was back in front of her, Veronica saw that her face was level with Dominique's pussy.

Dominique stepped back a little and took in the view of Veronica. Her round ass was sticking straight up in the air, her heaving breasts were fully revealed, her hands and feet were bound and spread-eagled, and her head was propped up. Veronica was totally exposed, vulnerable and ready to be used for Dominique's pleasure. Just the way she liked all her slaves. Dominique then slowly removed her thigh-highs and heels so Veronica could drink her in. Her large breasts shone in the light and her pussy glistened with moisture. Dominique walked back up to Veronica, grabbed her hair, pulled her head up slightly and guided her face hard into Dominique's waiting, wet snatch. Veronica willingly buried her mouth in Dominique's pussy. For someone that was inexperienced with other women, she instinctively knew what to do. Using her tongue to spread open Dominique's lips she worked it all around the exposed clit. Veronica instantly had a mouthful of Dominique's cum and lapped it up like a thirsty animal. She could not believe how big Dominique's clit was. It bulged out of its hood like a mini dick. So Veronica decided to suck on it as if it was one.

Dominique said, "There you go. Suck that clit and open your mouth. I am going to give you the nectar of your Goddess." As soon as she said that she let loose a massive squirt, spraying hot liquid all over Veronica's pretty face. As the next stream began to shoot, Veronica put her mouth completely around Dominique's pussy and drank every drop she could. Dominique squirted twice more and Veronica's face and chest were soaked until she was dripping with her Goddess's hot juice. Dominique looked down and saw a stream of her cum run down Veronica's tit and drip off her long nipple. Veronica continued licking and slurping until she took in the last drop of Dominique's essence.

Dominique laughed at the sight of Veronica strapped to The Hump, dripping wet with her cum. The girl had a dazed look on her face as if she did not know what had just happened to her. Dominique unstrapped Veronica's hands and gave her a Hitachi Wand. Veronica had seen the item before on a porn site, but did not know exactly what it could do. Dominique was about to show her. She spread her lips and told Veronica to place the head of the Wand right against her inner pussy lips. As the head went it, Dominique's large outer lips closed around it making a snug fit. Veronica switched it on and Dominique instantly began to quiver. "Turn it up. Full power, slave." Veronica switched it to the highest setting and Dominique began to shake with the eruption of pleasure in her throbbing pussy. She grabbed the young girl's hands and pulled her in to apply even more pressure. Dominique came over and over and when she released her hold on Veronica's hands, a great spurt of cum shot out for a few seconds in an arch like a fountain of water.

Veronica looked at Dominique in awe, amazed at how the woman was so powerfully orgasmic and in total control of her sexuality and body's biorhythms. Veronica now knew that she could squirt too, thanks to Dominique, and she longed to be a sex Goddess who could take maximum pleasure out of every encounter.

Dominique stood back up and decided to add a little humiliation to the game she was playing with Veronica, "Good girl, now crawl over to that table by the cabinet."

Veronica slid off The Hump and started to get up, when Dominique pushed gently down on her shoulders, making her bend over. Then she maneuvered Veronica down on all fours. "I didn't say stand up and go to the table, did I? I distinctly remember telling you to crawl to the table. Now, get over there and fetch my strap-on. The big black one for a little slut like you," and playfully slapped her ass.

Veronica dutifully crawled on hands and knees until she reached the table. She found a huge black strap-on there and picked it up. She was amazed that she might have to take it in her small tight pussy. It looked like it was easily eight-plus inches. She was still sore from fucking Brian. He had a great dick but not like this monster. She felt goose pumps sprout on her as she thought about the strap-on entering her. She turned around and began to crawl back to Dominique. She suddenly stopped when she saw her Goddess slowly shaking her head in disapproval.

Dominique said, "Put the cock fully in your mouth, then crawl over here." Veronica stuffed as much of the cock as she could down her throat and crawled with her head tilted back to hold the cock in place. When she made it to her Goddess, Dominique pulled the long black cock out and told her to strap it around Dominique's waist. When the strap-on was in place, Dominique looked like an exotically beautiful hermaphrodite with large luscious breasts, curvy ass, and a big black cock pointing straight up from a shaved black pussy.

Veronica was on her knees looking up at the shaft looming over her with trepidation. Dominique smiled and said, "Well, it's not going to suck itself." Veronica laughed and wrapped her lips around the enormous head and began sucking tenderly. Dominique said, "Is that how you sucked Brian's cock? No wonder he left you." This lit a fire under Veronica's ass and she began licking and sucking Dominique's cock like a champ. She spit her saliva all over the black monster to get it slippery and thrust her head up and down like a see saw with the strap on as the pendulum. Then she gripped it hard and tight and rifled the cock through her hand.

Dominique said, "Put it as deep in your mouth as it can go and look up at me the whole time." Veronica slobbered all over the cock and slowly ate it inch by inch, looking up at her Goddess as she did so. As she felt the cock hit the back of her throat, she protruded her mouth a little more forward to take the last inch and Dominique gave her a look of approval that she cherished.

Dominique said, "What a good little cocksucker you are! Now get back on The Hump and I will show you why I call it that." Veronica slid back onto the bench with her butt raised high in the air over the camel-like hump. Dominique stood on the leg posts that had special platforms on top for just such a position. She grabbed Veronica's ass cheeks and spread her pussy wide. A drop of fluid came out telling Dominique the girl was ready for her big black cock. Dominique touched the head of her cock to Veronica's engorged pussy lips and watched in fascination as the head forced them apart and slowly began inching its way forward. The lips parted and looked like a mouth opening wider and wider to take the intruding object deeper and deeper. Then as Dominique began thrusting in and out she marveled at the way the lips now looked like a mouth sucking on her cock. As Veronica moaned in pleasure with every thrust, Dominique realized the girl could take it and needed more. Dominique began slow and soft, but every time she pulled out, she pushed it back in a little harder and faster. Their fuck rhythm began to grow more intense and Dominique brought Veronica along inch by inch. After a few minutes of building up, Dominique was in full flight and pounding away on Veronica's pussy. For her part, Veronica clenched her teeth and gripped the hand posts as tight as she could just to hold herself steady as the pleasure rippled through her body. Dominique was fucking her hard and fast now and Veronica knew this was the culmination of her journey with Dominique that had begun a month ago. It felt so right, so pure and natural for her to submit to her Goddess and be fucked by her better than any man up until that point. She made the cry of love and screamed "I'm cumming! Goddess, I'm cumming!" Dominique looked down and saw Veronica's pussy juice leaking out around the edges of her strap on. Dominique knew her cock was acting like a plug holding back the deluge and so she pulled out to release Veronica's orgasm. The cum shot out right between Dominique's legs, who was impressed at the girl's volume and force of ejaculation. After the tremendous effort she just put out, Veronica collapsed against The Hump. Dominique saw Veronica go limp and she knew she had won. There was no willpower left in Veronica but total submission to her Goddess. Dominique watched as Veronica twitched and shook for five minutes trying to understand where she was and what had just happened to her.

Dominique nodded to herself. It had been a good session and Veronica would never be the same. However, it had been necessary. After all, a person cannot understand how to apply pain and pleasure unless she'd felt and understood the mutually reinforcing sensations herself. *That is, unless one is a Goddess*, thought Dominique, as she smiled in satisfaction.

Chapter 15

*T*he waitress placed the salad in front of Dominique and placed a chicken wrap down for Veronica. It was a week since the encounter between the two in the Dungeon. Their relationship had shifted since that night. Veronica would have attached herself to Dominique's hip if that were possible. Dominique kind of marveled at the change in the girl. She acted very much the sub for Dominique. She hung on her every word and acted as a sponge absorbing any advice, suggestions, and Dominique's overall attitude. Veronica's effort was not wasted. Because as subservient as she was to Dominique, her attitude to the rest of the world was anything but submissive. Dominique noticed a more assertive walk in the young woman as well as a marked difference in the way she talked to others. The old, shy Veronica seemed to be gone. A more mature woman had emerged from the Dungeon that day.

Even today, Dominique noticed the change. Since they'd found time to meet for lunch, Dominique appraised Veronica's work attire. She was wearing a black, fitted, pencil skirt, high-heeled black boots, and a deep-purple, silk blouse with one extra button opened. Her breasts puffed enticingly out of the top of her shirt and all of her make-up and jewelry tastefully rounded out her beauty. Dominique had arrived at the restaurant first today. She was able to watch the reactions of people when Veronica sashayed into the room. She had an aura of command about her now. Both genders eyed her as she came over, bent down, and hugged Dominique.

Last Friday night, Dominique had helped the broken Veronica get up off the table. She took her up to the guest bedroom and helped her get into its shower. Dominique set a couple of big fluffy towels on the sink for Veronica to find when she was done. Thinking the girl would stand under the water for quite some time, Dominique retreated to her bathroom to rinse off. As she put on her robe, she knew she had no qualms about what she just put Veronica through in the Dungeon. It was quite a turn-on for Dominique to thoroughly dominate the girl, and she thought Veronica would come out the other side of the experience a better woman.

When she had gone back into the guest bedroom, Veronica was laying down on her side with a smile on her face. When Dominique had walked over to the bed, Veronica reached up and wrapped her arms around Dominique. She hugged her for a full minute. Then without a word, she stood up and let the towels fall onto the floor. Completely nude, she turned around and pulled down the covers, climbed into the bed, and wrapped the blanket around herself. Dominique shut off the lamp and closed the door as she left.

Veronica slept for a long time. The next morning she woke up and found a new pair of jeans and a shirt that Dominique had arranged for a store to send over for her. Shuffling into the kitchen, she poured herself a cup of coffee and sat at the table with Dominique. After a quiet minute, she said, "Sorry, I am still processing everything that happened last night. That was my first time with a woman and it was incredibly intense." She broke into a small smile. "And my pussy has never felt this good before, despite being a little sore. I don't think I've had as many orgasms in my entire life as I did last night," she laughed.

Dominique laughed along with her. "I guess I was able to show you better than I could tell you."

"Well, it worked and you were right. I realize now that I jumped the gun with Brian. I should have been happy with a first date. I wasn't ready for all I tried to do with him, but now I know more than ever there is a Goddess awakening in me. The way I tried to dominate him felt natural but a little forced, and I think he sensed that. Last night taught me that I have a lot to learn. I am not going to try again with a man until I know I'm ready. Of course, a little input in that regard from my Goddess will be welcome."

Dominique smiled. "You aren't that far off, Veronica. I can tell by the gleam in your eye. I learned a lot, too. You have been an inspiration. I have in the back of my mind this idea of starting a service for women who want to empower themselves. I could unleash them both sexually and in their lives overall. I also know there are men who I can help to realize their submissive nature. I have not put all the pieces together yet, but the catalyst for the idea is there. Veronica, I have enjoyed watching you blossom, but I should have told you that you weren't ready to fly yet." They chatted some more over the course of the day until Veronica went back home.

It was back to work on Monday. The two of them had drinks for happy hour on Wednesday where Veronica peppered Dominique with all kinds of questions about dominating men. She was especially interested in knowing how to be in tune with her male subjects and when to push their limits or to ease up. Dominique realized she was starting to see a mature Veronica on the road to sophistication as a domme. She thought about patting herself on the back, but then thought it would look out of place in the restaurant.

Veronica interrupted her thoughts. "What are you smiling about?"

"Uh, it's a really good salad."

"Sure. So how has work been this week?"

"Same story, different day. The funny thing is I have increased my business since I got back from Chicago. The Dom guy I told you I met out there became an official client yesterday. So we had a staff meeting this morning and all of the praise was heaped on some of the men in the firm. I know one of the other women is doing almost as well as I am. And do you think they said anything to us? Nope! I am getting sick and tired of this good-old-boy's network."

"I see that same attitude in my office sometimes. I thought women were getting to the same level as men in this world."

"Depends on the company and the men. I have met some very enlightened men. I just don't have any heading up my firm. I feel like I'm at a crossroads."

"What are you going to do?"

"Trying to figure out my options. I could move to another company. With my record and clients, anyone would take me. But I'm afraid it would end up being the same church, different pew. I don't want to jump from one frying pan to another, or maybe directly into the fire."

"Have you given anymore thought to being a sexologist or whatever you want to call it, to other women?" asked Veronica.

"What do you think of the idea?"

"I think you have something there. I have been paying attention to other women this week. I can tell you that there are gals my age and twenty years older who could use your guidance. I'm grateful you took me under your wing, as I don't think you'd have trouble finding clients willing to pay."

"Hmm, that's good to know," said Dominique. "I can tell you that I have been giving it some serious thought. I even outlined a business plan. I'm thinking about doing it on a limited basis at first. But to be effective at it, I need some stability in my day job for a time. Right now, the crap I put up with at work is not making me feel stable there."

Veronica put her wrap down and said, "I know you'll figure it out. Probably in a very short while too. You are the most accomplished woman I've ever met. And you can't keep a good woman down!"

"You got that right," said Dominique. "I just have to put all the pieces together. So do you have any fun plans this weekend?"

"I have a cousin coming down this evening from New Jersey. We were close as kids and I'm going to show him around."

"Good for you. I think that sounds like a great idea," said Dominique.

"What are you up to?" asked Veronica.

"Birthday party tomorrow night for one of my friends. It should be a good time."

"If you have some time, maybe we can get together and talk next week. I haven't met any man that I am interested in, but I want to be ready when I do."

"Sure. I'm free on Tuesday. And don't worry, you'll be ready."

The women finished their lunch and left the restaurant. They hugged and said goodbye on the sidewalk and went their separate ways. As Dominique exited the elevator onto her floor, she caught the eye of one of the managing partners who was talking to one of her colleagues. He looked flustered and quickly scuttled away like a scared beetle as Dominique walked in his direction.

She sighed and shook her head at the poor excuse for the male gender that she was forced to work for. As she went into her office, Jaron and Travis followed her in. Jaron spoke first, "We heard what happened at the staff meeting. We think we work for the best person in this office and we detest that you do not get the respect that you should from management."

Dominique was touched by their concern. "It's an injustice, but I am making good money and building my resume, so when I leave the joke will be on them. What grapevine did you hear about the meeting from?"

"It wasn't a grapevine," said Travis, "it was Marcus. He came over and asked us how you were doing. He seemed really concerned. I think he is frustrated because out of all the people he oversees, you are the best. However, he knows you don't get the recognition you deserve."

"That's nice to hear. Of course, he wouldn't tell me that to my face, but I guess that's office politics. I am thinking about moving on to greener pastures."

Jaron said, "No way! We want to go with you no matter what. Why drive a Kia when you can stick with a Lexus?"

"We've actually discussed this," chimed in Travis. "We aren't going anywhere. You're stuck with us. Wherever you go, we go."

"Hey, guys, I am not stuck with you. We make a good team. I'll tell Marcus when I see him that I appreciate his concern."

"We mean what we said," said Jaron. "If, for whatever reason, you leave here and can take us, we'll go with you. Even if you open a lingerie shop."

Dominique laughed. "God, that's an image. I'll keep that in mind. Now go. Finish up and maybe we can get out of here early for a change."

The two young men actually bowed, turned on their heels, and went back to their desks. Dominique decided to plow through the stuff on her own desk. Getting out of work early today sounded like a really good idea!

An hour later, she had one more file to sort through and she could be on her way. Jaron buzzed her and said, "There is a Charles Simmons on the phone for you."

It took Dominique a second to put a face to the name. Then she smiled, picked up the phone, and said, "Hello, Charles. Did you call me for some pointers on shoes?"

She heard a hearty laugh on the other end, "No, but if I see any I like I may ask if I can model them for you."

"It is so nice to hear your voice again. I really enjoyed meeting you in Chicago."

"I did too," said Charles. "How's life in the nation's capital?"

"Life is terrific. How are you and your kids doing?"

"They're teens. I'm convenient when they need money, otherwise I am not to be seen with them." He chuckled. "That's unfair. We actually all get along pretty good. How is work going for you?"

"Not a great day to ask. I am doing very well by my clients, but I told you what it's like working in this office. I work my ass off, make the company money, and definitely feel underappreciated."

"Then this may be a timely call. I have been doing some checking up on you, young lady. I got a sterling report on your ability, integrity, and character. I also received more than a few comments that you were a natural leader."

"Checking up on me? Just how did you do that?"

"Dominique, I'm rich. It's easy. I also wasn't surprised by the leadership comments. I felt that quality resonate from you in Chicago."

"Why are you doing all of this?" asked Dominique.

"I'm starting the next phase of my company's growth," said Charles. "I am opening up two branch offices, one on the west coast and one in the east. I did many careful studies and I am not going the typical route of trying to open one in New York and one in Los Angeles. Instead, I am shooting for Washington DC and Seattle. I have the capital to start out with ten financial advisors in each place along with the appropriate support staff."

This news perked Dominique up. She liked Charles and he did not play favorites with whom he promoted in terms of gender. She had asked around about him while she was in Chicago and he had a good, solid reputation. He certainly was not one of the weasels that ran her firm.

"Then I am flattered by you asking around about me. Are you considering me for one of the advisor positions in your new office here in DC?"

"No," said Charles.

Dominique's stomach fell and she frowned.

"I want you," Charles continued, "to head up the office there."

It rarely happened, but Dominique was speechless. She wanted to say something, but nothing came out of her mouth.

Charles said, "Hello?"

The Goddess took over, "Charles, you took me completely by surprise. The timing of your call is so perfect. I learned more about your company after we met, and need to look over the particulars of what you want, but this sounds tremendously promising."

Charles replied, "I already have a contract, initial budget, and the guidelines we use for our office here ready to send you, if you are receptive to the offer. I don't like wasting a lot of time once I make up my mind."

"By running the office, you mean…"

"It's all yours. You will be a Vice President of my company and the contract outlines all of the financial considerations that pertain to that position. The budget will give you an idea of the initial capitalization you have available to find an office, and select a support staff and advisors. You will have some decent bait to dangle in front of advisors from other firms. You know the city and the area. This new branch of my company will sink or thrive by your efforts. Still interested?"

"I am intrigued." Dominique thought a second. "Charles, this has nothing to do with your admiration of my feet, does it?"

"Not exactly. First of all, I have a strict rule I impose on myself not to mix business with pleasure. That doesn't mean I don't enjoy joking and hanging out with my staff. But everyone always keeps their clothes on, so I am not talking about that kind of fun."

I wish he'd thought about that before we took our clothes off that night, Dominique thought to herself, but she said, "Good to hear. That's my work place philosophy too." She began thinking about the night she had emasculated this man. She had a vision of him in her pink crotch less panties, pink bra and playing with his clit at her command, and she almost burst out laughing. Fortunately, she was able to control it.

"I had a feeling you thought that way. I admit, I wrestled between offering you the position or asking you out, but needing someone in Washington to guide a new enterprise in town won out. I have to tell you, though; our talk in Chicago had a lot to do with this offer. I like my key people, whether male or female, to be comfortable in a leadership role. I know that you are."

"Charles, to say I am overwhelmed is an understatement. I am very confident I can do this and I relish the challenge. I just can't get over the timing. You send me the material you mentioned, and I'll examine it over the weekend. I can call you Monday with my decision."

"Sounds wonderful, Dominique. It should already be in your email."

Dominique turned back to her computer screen and saw an email from Charles at the top of her list. "It's there. You have a great weekend, Charles. I'll talk to you Monday."

"You too, Dominique. I hope you become a part of the team."

Dominique leaned back in her chair. Of all days to get such a call as this. The timing was perfect! It sounded exactly like the opportunity she wanted. The one thing that she would love to do is to show the ferrets that ran her company that she could outperform them in this city. For that matter, there were other men in the Washington financial community that she wanted to stick it to as well. She would thoroughly go over the information Charles sent her. In terms of her goals in the financial field, this was a great opportunity.

As the initial euphoria wore off, Dominique considered the freedom this new venture would give her. It would be a lot of work, especially in the beginning, but she would be the boss. Dominique knew that if she surrounded herself with the right people, she would succeed. In the time of one phone call, she had seen a career path open up for her that had seemed far off this morning.

Dominique also thought about her idea of being a sex therapist. After all, it was more of a vocation – something she wanted to do to empower other women. Doing it on a larger scale would enable her to fine-tune the method that worked best. After working with Veronica, Dominique knew this was something she had to do with her life.

This was a hell of an ending to the week. Dominique knew that she had a lot in store over the next year. All the possibilities excited her. She felt on top of the world, and more importantly, in control of her own destiny. Everything was in her hands and she did not want it any other way. She was all for helping women empowering themselves, especially herself, and she felt very empowered right now.

Her thoughts were broken by Jaron and Travis knocking and coming in to her office. Travis started to say, "We're all done and were wondering if we…" He stopped. "Why are you smiling like that?"

"Boys," Dominique said with her arms outstretched, "I know you can keep a secret. We are going to be packing our bags and heading out of here for greener pastures."

SYNOPSIS

This novel introduces the reader to Dominique La Belle, an incredibly sensual and educated woman who, as one of her lovers tells her, is a naturally dominating woman. This is a major part of her personality and it shows in business and in her relationships. She takes no prisoners whenever she finds a man worthy of her affections. That guy is in for the time of his life as long as he yields his passions to Dominique. If he does not realize who is in charge, she will quickly change his mind. Dominique is a Goddess, and every man had better know it! Entering Dominique's world is Veronica Cala, a young woman who believes she has the makings of a Goddess inside of her, but does not know how to access it. Dominique takes this waif under her wing and nurtures her in everything from fashion to making a mark in business to showing her how to have a man scream for more in the bedroom. It is the journey of an ugly duckling into a self-assured sexual swan.

Dominique is the total inspiration for Veronica's transformation. Dominique shares stories from her past; Reflections of a Goddess, The Awakening is an explicit and sensual

www.ingramcontent.com/pod-product-compliance
Lightning Source LLC
Chambersburg PA
CBHW051951090426
42741CB00008B/1345